Leaders at All Levels

Ram Charan

JB JOSSEY-BASS

Leaders at All Levels

Deepening Your Talent Pool to Solve the Succession Crisis

John Wiley & Sons, Inc.

Published by Jossey-Bass
A Wiley Imprint
989 Market Street, San Francisco, CA 94103-1741—www.josseybass.com

Wiley Bicentennial logo: Richard J. Pacifico

Readers should be aware that Internet Web sites offered as citations and/or sources for further information may have changed or disappeared between the time this was written and when it is read.

Limit of Liability/Disclaimer of Warranty: While the publisher and author have used their best efforts in preparing this book, they make no representations or warranties with respect to the accuracy or completeness of the contents of this book and specifically disclaim any implied warranties of merchantability or fitness for a particular purpose. No warranty may be created or extended by sales representatives or written sales materials. The advice and strategies contained herein may not be suitable for your situation. You should consult with a professional where appropriate. Neither the publisher nor author shall be liable for any loss of profit or any other commercial damages, including but not limited to special, incidental, consequential, or other damages.

Jossey-Bass books and products are available through most bookstores. To contact Jossey-Bass directly, call our Customer Care Department within the U.S. at 800-956-7739, outside the U.S. at 317-572-3986, or fax 317-572-4002.

Jossey-Bass also publishes its books in a variety of electronic formats. Some content that appears in print may not be available in electronic books.

Library of Congress Cataloging-in-Publication Data

Charan, Ram.
    Leaders at all levels: deepening your talent pool to solve the succession crisis / Ram Charan.
      p. cm.
    Includes index.
    ISBN 978-0-7879-8559-2 (cloth)
    1. Leadership. 2. Executive succession—Planning. I. Title.
HD57.7.C47374 2008
658.4'092—dc22
                                                     2007026429

Printed in the United States of America
FIRST EDITION

CONTENTS

Dedicated to the hearts and souls of the joint family of twelve siblings and cousins living under one roof for fifty years whose personal sacrifices made my formal education possible.

Leaders at All Levels

Rebuilding Succession and Leadership Development from the Ground Up

Crisis may be an overused word, but it's a fair description of the state of leadership in today's corporations. CEOs are failing sooner and falling harder, leaving their companies in turmoil. At all levels, companies are short on the quantity and quality of leaders they need.

There's no shortage of raw talent. Businesses could fill the leadership vacuum from their internal ranks if they knew how to spot and develop their real potential leaders. But they don't, despite the enormous resources and thought they pour into the task.

The first law of holes—when you're in one, stop digging—tells us what to do: abandon our traditional leadership development practices. They're not working. Tinkering and fine-tuning won't solve the fundamental problem. It's time for a completely new approach to finding and developing the kinds of leaders businesses need. That's what this book provides: a model for companies to reinvent their leadership development processes and for individual leaders to guide their own careers.

To fix the problem, you have to get to its root, which is the faulty conventional wisdom about what leadership is and how to improve it. I have some radically different, and doubtless controversial, views that are the foundation of the model presented here. Having observed how leaders develop, or fail to, over several decades, I have come to the following conclusions:

- *Not everyone can become a leader.* Leaders are different from everyone else in ways that no amount of classroom instruction can supply. Smartest, quickest, best performer—these and other superlatives are not useful in spotting those who have the raw talent for leadership. We have to stop using them. Leaders think and act differently. We can spot them if we know what to look for and sharpen our power of observation.

- *Leadership ability is developed through practice and self-correction.* People who have the talent for leadership must develop it. Their growth is accelerated when each new job lets them build their core capabilities and acquire new ones and when feedback is timely and precise. Repetitive practice of core skills hones judgment and paves the way for innovative ways to lead.

- *The CEO job requires giant leaps in learning.* Leaders will not be prepared to lead large companies unless each job is much more complex than the one before. Leaders must be immersed in complexity repeatedly in their careers. As they practice sorting through it, they learn to deal with it.

These tenets are the foundation of an approach to leadership development that focuses on spotting leaders early and putting them in situations that drive them to grow fast. The new approach transforms leadership development from a discrete activity run by the human resources staff to an everyday activity that is fully integrated into the fabric of the business and in which line leaders play a central role.

I call this approach the *Apprenticeship Model.* "Apprenticeship" may sound wrong for business executives, but it isn't. Apprentices are people who learn from doing, and that is precisely what the Apprenticeship Model provides: practice, feedback, corrections, and more practice. It is designed to give each promising leader the opportunities that are right for him or her at the fastest pace of growth he or she can handle, defining the learning needed in each new job and making sure the learning in fact took place before helping the leader take the next step or leap forward. With this approach, leaders develop increasingly sophisticated and nuanced versions of their core capabilities in an astonishingly short time.

You will need to know at the earliest possible time what a leader's true talents are. The first year is not too soon to start. Anyone with potential to be a leader is a "high potential." But the most critical need of a company is to build the talent pool from which the CEO comes. This is where you extract an ounce of gold from a ton of ore. A successful succession process must have an explicit component for identifying leaders early who could someday be a CEO and tailoring their experiences, training, and development to both their individual talents and to the demands of that most challenging job.

The Apprenticeship Model vests huge responsibility in line leaders who supervise other leaders. Preparing future leaders becomes part of their job description, executed with the same rigor as strategy, finance, marketing, operations, and regulatory compliance. But developing leaders is not their task alone. It is a companywide priority. People throughout the organization create jobs, lend their observations, remove obstacles—whatever it takes to keep leaders growing.

This model of leadership development is radical and not for the fainthearted. It requires profoundly different attitudes and mind-sets as well as major organizational changes, and the results don't come quickly. But it is eminently practical. It is based on decades of observation of hundreds of leaders in dozens of companies, ranging from small technology start ups to global giants like General Electric and Colgate-Palmolive from the American heartland to the middle of Mumbai. Is the effort worth it? Unquestionably. Companies that embrace the model or its tenets have built powerful talent engines that give them an edge.

This book provides concrete advice and real-world examples to help others make the change. It explains the processes and provides the tools that bring the Apprenticeship Model to life, as General Electric and Colgate-Palmolive have done and Novartis AG, Textron, and WellPoint, Inc., are doing. It is also a guide for aspiring leaders to develop their capabilities. Senior leaders bold enough to take it on will create a system and culture that continually strengthen leadership at all levels and that help them prepare for their own succession. This will be an enduring legacy.

Money, the primary focus of most business activities, is, after all, just a commodity. Leadership is a true differentiator and creator of value.

Chapter 1

A NEW WAY TO FUND THE LEADERSHIP TALENT DEFICIT

In 2004, as CEO Daniel Vasella mapped out the future of global pharmaceutical giant Novartis AG, he concluded that the company's ability to grow and achieve ambitious performance targets rested largely on the quality of its people, particularly its leaders. He stated it simply, "Better people produce better results," and worked closely with Juergen Brokatzky-Geiger, Novartis AG's head of human resources, to create processes, systems, and programs that would expand the depth and quality of the leadership pool.

The connection between developing leaders and Novartis's future soon became common wisdom companywide, and each of Novartis's divisions undertook leadership development efforts tailored to its unique challenges. Novartis Generics, formed by Sandoz's acquisitions of Hexal and Eon Labs in 2005, for instance, had to build a core of leaders who could position the business in the highly competitive generic pharmaceutical segment and develop the capacity to launch numerous products rapidly. The Vaccines and Diagnostics division, which had been formed after the acquisition of Chiron Corporation in 2006, had to establish the management style, culture, and leadership team that could take the merged organization forward.

Novartis Pharmaceuticals Corp., the U.S. affiliate of Novartis AG, faced a challenge of its own: fast growth and increasing complexity. It needed leaders with the capabilities to take it through years of momentous change.

The competition for talent had been intensifying for years, and Alex Gorsky, CEO of the U.S. affiliate, knew it would only get worse. He also knew that Novartis would need leaders with a range of capabilities, some of which differed from the current model its leaders were held up to. Markets were changing, and some segments that were relatively small in 2006 were expected to grow enormously. Public perception about health care and the political arena were also changing. Future leaders would need to be good at understanding the power shifts and decision makers' concerns.

The pharmaceutical market was also becoming more volatile. The introduction of a generic drug or a recall based on the FDA's shifting emphasis on caution over efficacy could wipe out revenues overnight and cause big shifts in product portfolio and strategy. Leaders had to be able to reprioritize on a dime. In addition, the pressure to develop and launch products quickly put a premium on collaboration across functions and divisions.

Recognizing the importance of leadership, Gorsky enlisted the help of Anish Batlaw, his head of HR, to take a hard look at Novartis's existing development practices, which differed across functions. The basic idea was right: find leaders and provide the right job experiences, supplemented with continuous learning opportunities. But the specifics of how decisions about leaders were made and on what basis varied. Typically, a manager seeking to fill a leadership job would write a job description, highlight the items that were most pressing, and then work with HR to select someone with those skills and capabilities. The individual's future leadership potential was not explicitly considered.

In addition, candidate assessments were generally performed by people within a functional area. A senior marketing person, for instance, might not think to include people from the sales organization when selecting a product director, even though he or she would have to work closely with sales. Similarly, marketing people would not be involved in choosing people for sales management jobs. Leadership talent planning also varied in the company; some areas of the business had successors in mind to fill leadership jobs that would open in the next few years while others had serious shortfalls.

Gorsky and Batlaw set out to sharpen every aspect of decision making around selecting and developing leaders. They extensively shared best practices across functions. For instance, one functional area had a systematic way of targeting up-and-coming leaders to fill slots that would open three to five years out, which became a model for others.

Novartis Pharmaceuticals U.S. first applied the new succession and leadership development approach to the vice president positions. The process began with analyzing the business and its context, defining its future needs, and working backward to sharpen the definition of high-potential leaders. Hitting financial targets and delivering business results would continue to be a necessary condition for promotion, but the ability to recognize patterns and shifts in the industry ahead of the competition became important, as did the ability to command the details and translate those details into higher-level strategic thinking. And because the company's growth trajectory meant the leadership ranks would continually expand, leaders would have to be able to build the company's capability and leadership bench strength by developing other leaders. Producing up-and-coming leaders who could help carry the company forward became an essential criterion.

It is common at Novartis for senior leaders to ask people specific questions about their work—whether it's the number of sales calls made on a particular product, or the market share in a certain segment—if only to gauge whether the person has command of the details of the job. The same attention to detail and facts is now applied to discussions of people's leadership ability. Focusing on facts and specifics adds rigor to the process of selecting and developing leaders.

Today the talent review process in Novartis Pharmaceuticals U.S. identifies the target job for an individual leader several years out, along with a development action plan to get him or her there quickly. If there's a big gap between the target job and the leader's current capabilities, Novartis asks, "What would happen if we put the person in the job right now?" then looks for ways to close the gap and thus minimize the risk, with assignments tailored to prepare the person. Before making any specific job assignments, however, many factors are considered, such as how to balance business needs (functional expertise or fit with the team composition) and personal needs.

Some individuals with leadership potential are given assignments in which senior leaders can observe them directly and meet with them individually to get to know them better. The senior leaders' insights become part of each individual's personalized development plan. Global assignments are encouraged to accelerate a potential leader's development, as is interaction with other Novartis businesses and leaders outside the pharmaceutical division.

The Novartis Pharmaceutical Corporation's leadership development program is one of many innovative programs across all the Novartis companies. CEO Dr. Vasella believes that future performance of the company is contingent on continued development of a high-quality talent pipeline.

Through continued refinement of its leadership development processes, he is confident that Novartis will better prepare and have the leaders it needs in 2010 and beyond—leaders at all levels who will be prepared to contend with the complexity and uncertainty that await them.

Leadership Development Is Broken

Leadership matters. It creates and harnesses the energy of people, gives them direction, and synchronizes their efforts. In fact, it is a leading indicator of a company's prospects, unlike financial results, which tell you only where the company has already been. Strong leadership makes a good company better just as surely as weak leadership lowers its prospects and over time ruins it.

Boards of directors and senior executives know this. They realize that the selection of a new CEO is one of the most important decisions a board ever makes and should be planned well in advance. They also understand that the quality of leadership at every level has a huge impact on the everyday running of the organization as well as on the pool from which CEOs are chosen. That's why many companies are willing to spend liberally on elaborate leadership development programs and why corporate boards have succession on their radar screens.

Yet, it's no secret that succession planning and leadership development fall woefully short in delivering on their promise. In a recent survey of board members, the consulting firm A. T. Kearney found that fewer than one in four directors believes his or her company's board is effective at developing leadership and planning for succession. Almost half of companies with revenues above $500 million have no meaningful CEO succession plan. Only a small minority of HR executives are satisfied with their companies' top-management succession processes. The consequences are well known: CEO turnover has increased sharply in recent years, with an increasing number being forced out of their jobs sooner rather than later.

Succession problems start with the overall leadership development process because that's where future CEOs ought to come from. Sometimes bringing in outside talent is the best solution to deeply embedded corporate problems. More often it is the *only* solution because the company has failed to produce the leaders it needs. Leaders recruited from outside cause needless disruption when they have trouble learning the business and the industry or adapting to or changing the culture. They import new teams and management styles that break down continuity and momentum, sap the energy for execution, and instill fear among employees. By the time the board realizes that its choice of CEO was a mistake or that the company is going in the wrong direction, competitors will have used the lost time to gain advantage.

Seeking a CEO from outside a company is not only risky but also getting harder and more costly. Shareholders have grown impatient with CEOs who don't perform, so boards are increasingly intolerant of mediocre performance and faster to dismiss chief executives—initiating yet another search. And there's new competition for the pool of talented CEOs from private equity firms, which can offer the best executives incredibly lucrative opportunities without the burden of having to satisfy multiple constituencies or undergo government scrutiny.

Nobody wins in the bidding war for leaders. Weaker companies find it difficult to compete for top talent and only grow weaker. Companies that are good at producing leaders must constantly struggle to retain the leaders they've grown. Fast-growing businesses struggle to build and retain the large and diverse pool of leaders they need to maintain their momentum.

We should read the severe shortage of leaders as an unmistakable sign that the typical approaches to leadership development are fundamentally flawed. Directors, CEOs, HR executives, and business leaders at all levels have not done well at selecting and developing other leaders. They don't seem to understand what makes a leader or what a leader's job entails. They focus on the wrong people for the wrong reasons. Many fail to recognize that developing other leaders is, or at least should be, a major part of every leader's job. They don't start until it is far too late to properly develop their leaders' capabilities to take a complex organization into a future fraught with rapid and destabilizing change.

In most companies, leadership development and succession planning are inconsistent and erratic, lacking discipline and regularity. In others, the discipline is there, but the substance is all wrong. People go through the motions of meticulously filling out forms and following procedures, but the methods for identifying and evaluating leaders are perfunctory and bureaucratic. Even companies that try to emulate General Electric, the paragon of executive leadership development, often go through the motions without applying the rigor and expertise that GE has developed.

You might think that the growth of graduate business programs in the past few decades has produced a huge pool of leaders ready to take the corporate reins. There's no question that many young people coming out of universities and business schools are quick thinkers, conceptually agile, facile with models and numbers, and able to diagnose a situation through data. They often show keen insight into business problems. Many are ambitious and driven. They want to succeed, and they impress their superiors with their analytical skills, PowerPoint presentations, and high energy. Their supervisors make a leap of faith and give these smart and aggressive young experts a shot at a leadership job based on those demonstrated analytical skills.

But analytical and presentation skills are only small components of leadership ability, and the gaps show up sooner or later. Some of these leaders are eliminated at various steps in their career paths, perhaps moving on to some other unsuspecting company. Others—a surprisingly large number—rise to senior positions. They may be promoted because they are outstanding functional experts or star performers in individual roles or as a reward for delivering results, but they haven't been assessed for their basic leadership talent. Even people who succeed as leaders within their functions are often misjudged and placed in high-level general management positions without ever having demonstrated the broad-based skills and experience such positions require. Good leaders do emerge from these flawed processes, of course, but it's often as a matter of luck. Ultimately, companies pay a price for the failure to recognize true leadership.

This doesn't have to happen. We know that it is possible for companies to build a steady stream of leaders and CEO contenders. Some—GE, Procter & Gamble, Colgate, PepsiCo, and Sherwin-Williams, among them—are net producers of senior leaders. If we learn the right lessons from these successes, we can incorporate the underlying principles into a new approach to leadership development and, with renewed effort, produce the kinds of leaders our corporations desperately need, including twenty-first-century CEOs.

Although top leaders may be in short supply now, there is no shortage of raw talent. Michelangelo turned a block of marble into the breathtakingly beautiful *Pieta* because he had the talent. Similarly, a talented leader can take an otherwise shapeless organization and mold it into a highly efficient, highly motivated force for innovation and growth. It is good business sense and practically a moral oblig-ation to identify and unleash those talents. Companies can grow all the leaders they need and then some once they think clearly about what a leader truly is and what's required to develop one and then take decisive action to shape their leadership gene pool.

How to Develop a Leader

We know that leadership development does happen, often ad hoc: for instance, when a seasoned leader takes a special interest in a junior person and provides that person with the experiences and coaching to help him or her flourish. Those isolated cases are often brilliant demonstrations of what our leadership development processes ought to accomplish. The disguised but real story of Bob and Gary is a case in point.

Bob had risen to the level of executive vice president of sales and marketing at his company, a global consumer durables manu-facturer, and had hopes of becoming the CEO. As it turned out, someone else was chosen. Bob nevertheless stayed on, and the new CEO was wise enough to make full use of his skills. He gave Bob considerable latitude to allocate marketing resources and sought his advice on other matters as well, almost as if Bob were in the role of chief operating officer.

While rightly proud of his accomplishments in sales and mar-keting, Bob believed that the best legacy he could leave his com-pany was to begin developing a new generation of leaders. Setting out to find, recruit, and nurture executive talent, he started by searching among the best business schools and consulting firms for promising young people, hoping to interest them in a career at the global manufacturing company whose products were part of the daily lives of millions of people. Although he didn't commit it to paper, he had a clear idea of what he was looking for: broad thinkers, fast learners, people with the ability to get along with dif-ferent kinds of people in different cultures, the ability to think ana-lytically as well as creatively and intuitively, a strong character, a drive for excellence, and a desire to help others succeed. He found half a dozen such people in their early or midtwenties and brought them into corporate headquarters where he could personally work with them and assess their talents. His plan was to then deploy them in various parts of the company where their talents seemed to fit, not just sales and marketing.

Gary made a particularly strong impression on Bob. He soaked up everything around him, worked well with everyone he interacted with, always asked great questions that went beyond the boundaries of his particular assignment, and sometimes unearthed problems in the making. Within two years, Bob dispatched him to run the sales and marketing operation in Brazil, an important and growing market for the company.

Brazil was far from headquarters, but Bob made a habit of staying in close contact with all the young leaders he placed, as well as with their bosses. He monitored their performance and talked to them often, giving advice and acting as a sounding board on various business issues that arose. He talked to Gary about dealing with distributors, observing consumer behavior, and understanding the impact of currency fluctuations on the business, and he occasionally tested Gary's imagination with provocative questions such as "What could headquarters do to bring its Brazil operation to number one in market share?" Business issues aside, living and working in a country with a different culture and language were a challenge for Gary. But he rose to the occasion, learning fast, cementing relationships with the company's distributors and retailers, and boosting sales 10 percent in each of the two years he held the post.

The Big Leap to Profit-and-Loss Responsibility

With Bob acting as his representative at headquarters, Gary's performance came to the attention of other senior executives. When his boss returned to the United States for his next assignment, Gary was among the candidates who were marked as potential replacements. He was considerably younger than any other candidate and had no profit-and-loss (P&L) experience, as others did. Some executives at headquarters thought it was too much of a jump to put him in charge of a P&L operation as large as that in Brazil. But Bob had seen Gary grow and knew that his knowledge base, relationships, and perspective had expanded beyond the current job. He had a sense that Gary had only begun to reveal his capacity to grow. He brought Gary's qualities into focus for the top team, and the CEO agreed to give Gary a chance.

There was no question that running the entire Brazil operation was an enormous undertaking, but during his two years in sales and marketing, Gary had laid the groundwork, making it a point to get to know people in the company's manufacturing, purchasing, governmental affairs, and HR departments. His obvious interest in what they did created an environment of goodwill that became an important source of support and encouragement as he delved into the myriad business details and relationships that are the hallmark of a complex manufacturing and marketing company. Over the next three years, Gary cut costs, increased productivity, oversaw the introduction of new products, and gained market share against the company's major competitors.

While Gary was learning to run the Brazil business, trouble was brewing thousands of miles away. A few years earlier, the company, eager to get a foothold in the lucrative Japanese market, had bought a sizable minority stake in a Japanese competitor. But the Japanese company was faltering. Its manufacturing operations were inefficient, its products weren't keeping pace with shifting consumer preferences, and its management didn't seem to know what to do about the problems. Bob and Gary's CEO faced a major decision: either abandon the Japanese investment or become more deeply involved in managing it. He preferred to try to salvage the relationship if he could and persuaded his Japanese partner to accept a veteran manufacturing executive, Tony, as CEO of the joint venture. Before he left for Tokyo, though, Tony made it clear that he wanted someone strong in sales and marketing to go to Japan with him.

"Let's send Gary," Bob suggested to the CEO. "He knows the business, he's proven himself in a foreign culture, and he has the people skills to work with a diverse group. If anybody can do it, he can." The CEO wasn't sure. The Japanese did everything by seniority, and whereas Tony had years of experience, Gary was still only in his early thirties. More important, the Japanese management might balk at two Americans telling them how to do things. But the CEO knew Bob's opinions of up-and-coming leaders were informed and objective. When it came to gathering information about his young protégés, Bob left no stone unturned. He cross-checked his own opinions and was always willing to change his views. When Bob saw other young leaders fail to acquire certain capabilities he'd hoped they would, he guided them into jobs that played to their particular talents. He believed, and other people confirmed, that Gary was a born general manager and relationship builder with great adaptability to different cultures. In the end, the CEO was convinced, and Gary was offered the job.

Moving Forward by Stepping Back

Now Gary faced a quandary. He was running an important country operation, in charge of every aspect of the business. He was being offered a sales and marketing job. "Been there, done that," he thought to himself. In a weekend telephone call to Bob, Gary worried that the Tokyo job would be a move backward. Maybe it was better to wait for another line job to open up, perhaps back in the United States.

"Take it," Bob counseled. "Don't worry about titles and hierarchy. Japan isn't anything like Brazil; you'll be working with a different company that has its own culture and methods, and the market there is huge. I guarantee you it will be a stretch. You won't get bored, and you'll learn a lot."

Everything about Japan was different from anything Gary had ever done before. Accustomed to noisy, good-humored debate among his Brazilian colleagues, Gary found the Japanese executives eerily silent in meetings. The sales staff didn't communicate with their marketing peers, and neither connected with manufacturing or product design. There were too many people in every department. They seemed to be working hard, but not much seemed to get done. Gary had to fall back on his people skills to begin drawing out the staff at meetings and in one-on-one encounters.

His biggest challenge at first was to get differences of opinion in the open. The Japanese respect for elders and the pervasive politeness stifled any dissent. Some of the younger marketing people had good ideas for reaching out to a younger customer base, but they rarely presented those ideas at meetings. Gary had to repeat time and again that debate was healthy and that ideas that were challenged would become better as a result. Gradually the meetings began to flow more freely.

Even as he was laboring to spark enthusiasm among his staff, Gary was establishing relationships in other parts of the company. He visited the factories, talked to product developers, and invited retailers to sake-drenched dinners. Such forays revealed a good deal about the company, including the fact that his boss, Tony, wasn't having much success insinuating himself into the company's management structure. Although Gary's efforts were gradually showing results in market share, other necessary changes weren't happening. That was becoming evident back at headquarters, too. Two years after he took the post, Tony was recalled to the United States, and the debate about what to do about Japan started all over again. Bob knew that Gary had been learning and building relationships in Japan beyond his sales and marketing responsibilities and urged the discouraged CEO to let Gary make a presentation about what was wrong there and what could be done to fix it. The CEO agreed to have Gary address the board at its next meeting as a prelude to making a decision about which way to go in Japan.

Gary laid out the basics to the board: an unfocused workforce, somewhat outmoded and excess capacity, products that lacked a strong differentiation and consumer appeal, and a demoralized and uncommunicative leadership. The leadership at several levels, he told the board, was the real root of the problem. If they could be inspired to work together like his own sales and marketing team was working, they could solve the other problems systematically. He told the board that he believed that the Japanese business was worth saving. The market was huge and growing and could become a platform to move into other parts of Asia.

The Leap to Strategy

By this time, Gary had a reputation within the company as a strong communicator with the ability to make the right decisions without delay. Although his strategic thinking was untested, his grasp of the Japanese situation was compelling. There was little debate among the board members when the CEO suggested that Gary be put in charge of the Japanese joint venture for one last attempt to salvage the company's investment.

As head of the Japanese company, Gary called on many of the skills and insights he had gained in previous jobs, but setting the strategic direction for such a large and pivotal operation was new territory for him. He knew that the Japanese were excellent at execution, but for any changes to occur he would have to energize his team of senior executives in adherence with the Japanese consensus-building culture. He would need to take the business in a markedly different direction and create a shared commitment to it so that people would be willing to tackle the drastic steps required, including closing one or more factories and sharply reducing staff. Finally, the executives had to develop a shared view of the possibilities and opportunities the company could seize, first in Japan and later throughout Asia.

When Gary laid out to his leadership team his analysis of the company's problems and the changes he had in mind, everyone seemed afraid to make suggestions or even ask questions. He was encouraged when individuals began dropping by his office to bring up their concerns and urged them to speak up about those concerns in the next meeting. A few did, but what really turned the tide was when Gary found a way to make the Japanese more comfortable discussing ideas and posing questions. He made a presentation to them, laying out the financial picture for the company. He then broke the leaders into groups of three or four and asked them to discuss—in Japanese, if they preferred—some ideas to solve the problems. The informality of the small groups and use of Japanese helped people be more candid, and focusing on the business as a whole eased tensions. The executives had never seen the numbers for the overall business before; typically, each executive focused on the numbers for his area. After an hour or so, the groups met together, and a spokesperson for each summarized their discussions.

Six months into Gary's tenure as CEO, the change among the senior executives was palpable. Not only were they asking the kinds of sharp questions that indicated they understood the overall picture, they began debating one another in front of the entire group. Gary had found a way to make a huge change in the culture.

Two years after he took over the company, Gary had set it on course to profitability with a fresh consumer orientation, new product offerings, efficient manufacturing, and a lean staff. Over the next three years, he continued to expand the company's market share in Japan, entered new markets in Asia, and repaired the company's balance sheet. The company became a net cash generator. He also oversaw the creation of a leadership development process that, while taking into account Japan's seniority-based promotion practices, identified leadership talent early and set those young people on paths that would challenge them and expand their capabilities. That ensured the operation would thrive after he left.

Gary continued to expand his capabilities while he was running Japan: he attended one-day seminars to stay abreast of external trends; learned how to deal with Japanese investors, financial markets, and unions; and built networks with CEOs of other companies. He continued to find Bob's occasional fifteen-minute phone calls stimulating, when Bob would ask, "What are you working on now?" or "What's new since we last talked?" or "What's your current challenge?" Those simple questions prompted Gary to distill his learning.

Bob retired just before Gary was recalled to U.S. headquarters as executive vice president. Gary left behind a stronger business in Japan. The organization was energized and on track, and he could confidently recommend to the board that he be succeeded as CEO of the joint venture by the Japanese company's chief operating officer (COO). The COO, an engineer by training, had been inspired by what he saw Gary accomplish and three years earlier had taken it on himself to study finance to broaden his understanding of the company. Nearly three years later, the business continues to meet its heightened financial targets.

Bob took risks on Gary with every move, but they were all based on deep knowledge of Gary's leadership skills, personal traits, and performance. At every turn, Bob was vigilant in seeking hard evidence of how Gary was progressing. He guided Gary but never dictated what he should do. He asked questions that opened Gary's mind and made suggestions in Gary's best interest. Not that Gary played a passive role in his success. He recognized early in his career that he, more than anyone else, would be responsible for developing his leadership skills and took every opportunity to do so, even if it meant making an unconventional career move.

It's too soon to tell whether Gary will become a CEO either at his company or somewhere else, but he continues to thrive in his current job running the company's largest and most important division. What's not in question is that both Gary and the company benefited immensely from Bob's efforts to develop his protégé's leadership talent, help him identify the right next job, coach him to improve his performance in the job and prepare for the next one, and bring his particular strengths into sharp focus.

Don't Leave Leadership Development to Chance

Consider why some would say Gary was lucky: his potential was recognized early. He was not subjected to perfunctory, bureaucratic performance reviews but was assessed broadly by a mentor who was deeply familiar with his activities and knew him well as a person. He had someone pushing other executives to give him the opportunities to make big moves rather than stepping up prescribed, incremental rungs. Each job was a stretch that enhanced his existing talents and honed core capabilities while also allowing him to develop new ones. He received personal feedback and coaching. And his growth was in the hands of a committed, seasoned leader who measured his own success in part, and in this case voluntarily, by Gary's.

These are precisely the elements that any young person with CEO potential can benefit from, and they are what we should try to embed in our approach to leadership development. Companies have to ensure that potential leadership talent, wherever it resides, is spotted early and developed thoroughly to create a corporate talent pool that is capable of leading in an environment not yet foreseen. Those with potential to succeed at the highest levels should be allowed to spread their wings early and encouraged to move in big leaps through a variety of challenges tailored to their particular strengths and developmental needs. Their progress must be closely watched to see what talents are proving out and what limitations might be emerging. And they need ongoing feedback on every aspect of leadership but, most important, on the business issues and people side—not just their leadership style—by leaders who have business savvy and are close to their everyday work.

Imagine if all high-potential leaders underwent such customized development. The results could be profound. Rising leaders, unshackled from stifling bureaucracy, would grow at the fastest pace that their capabilities would allow. Those leaders would become agents of change: fundamentally altering the nature of the company by seizing hitherto unrecognized opportunities and energizing the company's competitive instincts. The pool of management talent would be diverse and therefore well prepared to cope with changing conditions in markets and the competitive environment. Certainly some leaders would reach the limits of their capabilities below the CEO level, but leaders at all levels would be making the most of the talents they have.

Our current formalistic processes and training programs will not get us where we need to be, no matter how much we spend on them, because they are built on serious misconceptions about leadership and its development. These shortcomings include

- Failing to recognize that only a few people have the potential to run a major company and that these people must be spotted early to spare them the torture of having to prove themselves at every rung in a ten-step vertical ladder.
- Failing to make the identification and development of other leaders an explicit part of every leader's job and to provide the tools to do it and the rewards for doing it well. Companies track a leader's ability to produce numbers but not her ability to produce other leaders.
- Relegating the early identification and development of high-potential leaders to lower-level leaders who are ill prepared for the task.
- Using perfunctory and bureaucratic "performance reviews" as a coaching and career-planning device.
- Applying the same expectations and job rotations to all leaders, rather than customizing them to an individual's talents and developmental needs.
- Spreading leadership development resources across too many leaders in hopes that strong ones will emerge.
- Using classroom education as a substitute for real-world challenges.

Leadership Development Requires Radical Change

The need for a new approach to leadership development is clear. The "how" is not so obvious. The following chapters explain it. As you read on, you will discover a new model for succession and leadership development, one that will help you build a stream of leaders at all levels. If you do this, you will also largely solve your CEO succession dilemma. No matter how refined the process for selecting a CEO or how diligently the board works to choose the right one, the odds of success are far higher when it has a robust process and a substantial internal pool of leaders at all times to choose from.

Does Your Company Know How to Develop Leaders for the Highest Levels?

Rate your company on a scale from one to ten.

1. Developing other leaders is an important part of every leader's job at my company. Leaders are expected to devote considerable energy and a minimum of 20 percent of their quality time to it.

   Not at all true   ⟶   Definitely true

1	2	3	4	5	6	7	8	9	10

2. Leaders who identify and develop other leaders are rewarded and recognized for doing so.

1	2	3	4	5	6	7	8	9	10

3. Bosses regularly coach leaders on the one or two most important things they need to improve, such as specific aspects of business acumen or relationship skills.

1	2	3	4	5	6	7	8	9	10

4. Evaluations at least once a year consider not just what the leader achieved but also *how* and under what circumstances.

1	2	3	4	5	6	7	8	9	10

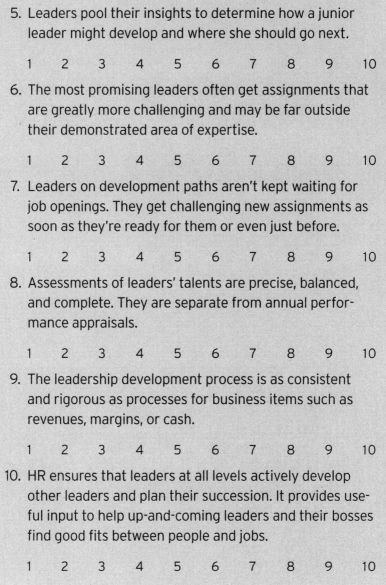

5. Leaders pool their insights to determine how a junior leader might develop and where she should go next.

    1   2   3   4   5   6   7   8   9   10

6. The most promising leaders often get assignments that are greatly more challenging and may be far outside their demonstrated area of expertise.

    1   2   3   4   5   6   7   8   9   10

7. Leaders on development paths aren't kept waiting for job openings. They get challenging new assignments as soon as they're ready for them or even just before.

    1   2   3   4   5   6   7   8   9   10

8. Assessments of leaders' talents are precise, balanced, and complete. They are separate from annual performance appraisals.

    1   2   3   4   5   6   7   8   9   10

9. The leadership development process is as consistent and rigorous as processes for business items such as revenues, margins, or cash.

    1   2   3   4   5   6   7   8   9   10

10. HR ensures that leaders at all levels actively develop other leaders and plan their succession. It provides useful input to help up-and-coming leaders and their bosses find good fits between people and jobs.

    1   2   3   4   5   6   7   8   9   10

Chapter 2

HOW APPRENTICESHIP TURNS POTENTIAL INTO LEADERS

It's hard for most people to picture a corporate executive as an apprentice, someone whom the dictionary defines as engaged in learning a skill or a craft. But the concept of apprenticeship is at the heart of this new approach to leadership development. To understand why, you'll have to come to grips with a potentially controversial belief: leadership can only be developed through practice. People can pick up tools and techniques and ideas about leadership from a book or a classroom. A lot of what passes for leadership development consists of this sort of thing. But those who have a talent for leadership must develop their abilities by practicing in the real world and converting that experience into improved skill and judgment. That conversion does not take place in a classroom, and not everyone can make that conversion. I have reached this conclusion after several decades of working with leaders at all levels in all kinds of companies.

Let's take it down to the ground level. An apprentice system doesn't waste time trying to teach, say, a man with no mechanical abilities how to operate a complex machine tool. It starts with one who has that inherent aptitude and develops his skills over time. He may have some book and classroom training, but the art and skill that he learns working with seasoned technical people is what will someday make him a master toolmaker. Business leadership is no different. Leaders—meaning those people with the inherent aptitude of leadership—develop predominantly through experience, combined with substantive evaluation and self-correction along the way.

The Apprenticeship Model is a rigorous system for providing experiences and feedback that are tailored to accelerate each leader's development. It starts by identifying the people who show signs of leadership aptitude. These are the people we call *high-potential leaders*. The model pinpoints each leader's specific talents and identifies some who are likely to have the highest potential—the qualities that could make some of them good CEOs down the road.

Companies using the model put leaders in jobs carefully chosen to build on their existing talents and test their ability to discover or acquire new capabilities. They also provide feedback in real time so the leaders continually improve their skills and judgment. At least once a year, their companies review the learning that has taken place and identify the learning that must come next for each leader to build his own brand of leadership. They take risks on leaders deemed to have the highest potential by putting them in jobs that are immensely more complex than the one before, giving them the practice they will need to someday make the leap to CEO.

In the Apprenticeship Model, leaders at every level not only have to develop their own leadership capabilities, they must at the same time play an essential role in identifying and developing other leaders' talent, particularly for the people who report directly to them (their "direct reports"). This is a new way of looking at a leader's job and will require a different mind-set and often some new skills for leaders throughout the organization.

Accelerating the development of each leader's talent not only strengthens leadership at every level, which is important in its own right, but it also lays the foundation for a robust CEO succession process. Moving up incrementally through an organization does not prepare a leader for the scope and complexity a CEO must contend with. We will return to the subject of developing CEO talent later in this chapter and again later in the book.

Key elements of the Apprenticeship Model, then, are to define leadership potential correctly, spot it as soon as possible, then focus time and attention to help talented young leaders develop through a series of jobs customized to allow each one of them to expand as quickly as possible. Leaders at every level participate actively in growing other leaders, and leadership development becomes a key component of every leader's job. That's how the Apprenticeship Model transforms an organization into a self-perpetuating leadership development machine.

What follows is an overview of the model. Each component will be explained more fully in later chapters.

Identify Leadership Talent Early and Correctly

Finding leadership talent early is essential. The path from initial recruitment to the senior levels of a company is approximately twenty-five years long and involves, on average, only five jobs before becoming eligible for the CEO post. Most high-level job incumbents reach that point by the age of about fifty. The sooner potential talent is identified, the better it can be developed and tested. Finding the *right* talent is equally important because growing high-potential leaders is highly resource intensive. The most precious resources here are not financial but the time, energy, and attention of other leaders. These are always in short supply and must therefore be devoted to the people who are most likely to succeed at top levels.

Spotting leaders early means spotting them in their very first jobs. Leaders at lower organizational levels must learn how to identify people who have a talent for leadership, however undeveloped it is. Senior leaders must work with these lower-level leaders to ensure that the identification process is working as it should.

The essence of early identification is to find people with a natural talent to lead and, importantly, to understand business. A keen observer can usually spot that talent by the time a person is twenty-five years old and is entering the workforce. A high-potential candidate will exhibit the drive to master new skills, the ability to rapidly absorb knowledge and then communicate it, and a natural bent to build lasting relationships and mobilize others to get things done. He will be learning not only what his own job entails but what his boss's job and his boss's boss's job requires. He will invariably redefine his own job, sometimes explicitly and deliberately, and in doing so may force his boss to rethink his own job as well. By definition, a high-potential person will outshine his bosses until this person reaches his full potential, and the leadership of a company needs to be aware of that dynamic. No forty-five-year-old will become the CEO of a major company unless he outshines every boss from the time he enters the company until he is nominated for the job.

The leaders with the highest potential will have what I call "the CEO nucleus," the intuitive ability to comprehend the total picture of a business and how it makes money in the language of a street vendor. Another essential is the ability to work with and motivate people, and a third is the intellectual capacity to see ambiguous, complex, nonquantifiable situations from a broader view and through several different lenses.

Planning the Apprenticeship for Fast Growth

Once a high-potential candidate has been identified, his fundamental development is done through a series of what can be described as planned apprenticeships. If a person is to become a high-level leader by age forty-five and stays in each job for three to five years (long enough to learn the job and to show results), there will be on average just five jobs between entering the workforce and assuming a top leadership job. The content of those jobs, and therefore their design or selection, is crucial. The company and the individual need to maximize the developmental value of each job to test and expand developing leaders on multiple levels, including their business judgment, their psychology, their ability to get others to do what must be done, and their ability to learn and grow.

One-size-fits-all career paths and prescribed rotations through business functions or geographical locations do not create the kinds of leaders needed in the twenty-first-century corporation. Sometimes leaders get moved through positions too quickly for anyone to know how well the person really performed or to fully immerse the person in a different culture. Often the jobs are repetitive or simply not enough of a stretch. Incremental steps in scope and complexity are too slow and will not prepare the person for what she'll face at higher levels. Besides, lacking a challenge, such a person may well become bored and seek bigger opportunities elsewhere.

Rather, careers must be managed in a way that allows leaders to grow with a pervading sense of urgency. Each job given a high-potential leader must be a stretch that develops her natural leadership talents and tests her ability to develop new skills and capabilities and to refine her personal traits.

The Boss as Mentor

When a leader doesn't develop despite having been nurtured through jobs of increasing responsibility, you have to ask why not. Was she not equal to the challenge? Did she not get the right kind of guidance? Did she fail to refine her abilities and judgments? Experience becomes learning only when the leader makes adjustments based on insightful feedback, intelligent self-reflection, or both. Some leaders—the Horatio Alger types—develop largely on their own, instinctively making corrections to their behavior and judgment, but most will improve faster with the help of a mentor who provides timely, insightful feedback.

As in any organization with a good leadership development process, bosses carefully observe the leaders and give feedback and coaching. In the Apprenticeship Model, the boss as mentor takes a close personal interest in guiding and developing his young leaders, helping them to broaden their thinking, sharing his experience and wisdom, and digging deep to pinpoint each leader's specific talents. That's why the mentor and the boss should be one and the same. Bosses see people in action, observe their behaviors, and know the leader as a whole person. They can evaluate the quality of their decisions in the context of the particulars of a situation and provide coaching and feedback in real time. Leaders at every level must expand their jobs to include accelerating the development of other leaders. They must raise their observational acuity and change their mind-set about what they're looking for in leaders—not just an ability to exceed stated objectives, for instance, but also a leader's natural talents and true potential.

Some bosses will be better at this role than others, but those who don't have the interest or mentality to observe a subordinate's actions, decisions, and behaviors; give feedback and coaching; and make incisive observations and judgments about the person shouldn't be bosses.

Even the best mentor-boss can't do the job without the help of senior leaders and human resources. The most complete and nuanced picture of a leader comes from inputs of many people. Those collective insights help detect the trajectory of a leader's growth and inform decisions about where the leader should go next.

Challenges in Executing the Model

It should be clear by now just how different the Apprenticeship Model is from conventional approaches to identifying and developing leaders. (The chart shown in Figure 2.1 captures these differences.) Adopting and executing it will require committed effort because it involves changing the way people think and act throughout the organization. You have to accept that truly high-potential leaders are different from other people and warrant the disproportionate share of time and attention. At the same time, you have to be clear that although leaders are different from other people, they are not superior human beings. Businesses need to change their thinking about leadership as the pinnacle of success for everyone and stop doling out leadership jobs as rewards for people who perform very well but simply are not leaders. Companies should instead see leadership for what it is: a distinct job that requires distinct talents that not everyone has to the same degree.

Understand that results will take years, not weeks or months, to materialize. A company that does not already have a functioning leadership development model can expect to spend from two to three years getting the new system and culture fully established,

Figure 2.1 Key Differences Between Conventional Leadership Development and the Apprenticeship Model

Conventional Leadership Development

- Focus on inputs: classroom hours, money spent, "our own Crotonville"

- Required resources: mostly money

- Development resources spread thin

- HR in charge of developing leaders

- Universal set of competencies and traits for all leaders

- Incremental linear upward moves

- Emphasis on classroom training and "exposure"

- Waiting for jobs to open and charting standardized career tracks

Apprenticeship Model

- Focus on output: are we getting the leaders we need? "our own pool of CEO succession candidates"

- Required resources: mostly leaders' attention and emotional energy

- Resources focused disproportionately on a smaller, high-leverage group of leaders

- HR as trustee of leadership developement; bosses play central role in developing leaders

- Defining each leader's individual talent, skills, and personal traits

- Leaps up several rungs or levels of complexity; some horizontal moves

- Emphasis on "deliberate practice"

- Creating or redesigning jobs tailored to each leader's developmental needs depending in part on how aggressively senior management pushes and how insistent the human resources function is in getting the program implemented.

Adopting this model begins at the top of the company. Leadership development should be an integral part of both the company's mission and vision statements. More important, the CEO and HR must create a basic methodology that provides recognition, rewards, and punishment for the top team based on its ability and commitment to drive leadership development. The top team sets the example for everyone else and has to be reviewed and rewarded appropriately. Finally, the company must redefine roles and create the processes and mechanisms to execute the leadership model.

Some busy executives may object that they don't have the time to take on the mentoring role. Hard as it may be to believe, making judgments about the leaders who work for you doesn't take extra time. It's a matter of what to focus on in the ordinary interactions with people. True, it takes extra thought, but that, too, becomes routine in time. The bigger obstacle is whether the boss has the requisite personal traits. It requires psychological fortitude to push rising young leaders ahead of you. It also requires the creativity and will to imagine what young leaders might become and where they will flourish. Finally, it takes courage to unblock jobs by moving people out of them so that high potentials get opportunities to gain necessary experience. Compensation should reward or punish leaders according to their ability to develop more leaders. Bosses who don't have what it takes to develop leaders or don't want the responsibility should be coached, but if they're unwilling to change, they must be replaced.

The recruitment process will change, too. Young people entering the organization will be intensely scrutinized to determine if they have the innate talents to become leaders. Many who think they do will fail that scrutiny. They may choose to leave, but they might also be persuaded to stay and make strong individual contributions if they're given the right motivations and compensation. The recruitment of midlevel and higher executives must include the ability to develop other leaders as a nonnegotiable criterion.

Although line managers and senior managers are the corner-stone of this development process, the HR function is in no way diminished. To the contrary, HR is the *trustee* of the Apprenticeship Model. Just as the company looks ahead to do capacity planning for its hard assets, HR looks ahead to ensure that the company is creating and developing a leadership pool for the future. The HR role at every level is to be sure the leadership development process is working effectively to produce robust outcomes and to contribute to discussions of leaders and their particular paths.

The Apprenticeship Model imposes heavy responsibilities not only on the company and its existing leaders but also on the high-potential leaders themselves. They need to take personal responsibility for developing their talents and judgment and mastering skills. They bear ultimate responsibility for choosing the right jobs, calibrating their bosses as good mentors, and evaluating the context and ambiance in which they work. If a job isn't right, the global shortage of talent ensures plenty of other opportunities. But individuals who aspire to leadership at higher levels must appreciate the value of constructive feedback and combine it with self-awareness and a desire and drive to improve. The pace of their learning must match their ambition.

All this disruption and change will lead to more powerful, energized leadership at every level of the organization. And the biggest payoff will come the day the board has to name the next CEO. That person will have been tested and proven on the way up and will be able to take the company forward into whatever changing environment it may face—even as several other potential successors are being groomed.

Choosing the Next CEO

Filling the CEO job is the ultimate challenge of any succession and talent development system; it takes a ton of leadership ore to produce an ounce of CEO gold. General Electric, the quintessential developer of leaders, had some 225,000 workers in 1993 when Jack

Welch identified twenty-two potential successors: four he categorized as "most likely," six "probably," and twelve "long shots." Over the next seven years, he eventually winnowed the twenty-two down to just three. Any company developing its high-potential leaders must carefully sort the few with CEO potential from the many likely to be good at leading projects, departments, business units, functions, divisions, or regions. To do that, people must fully understand what it takes to be a CEO.

The job of a CEO is more intellectually, socially, politically, and psychologically demanding than ever. And it is much more challenging than other jobs leading up to it. It requires courage and character but also the mental ability to understand numbers and at the same time to do qualitative reasoning that transcends the numbers. It is a juggling act not just in time and attention but in much deeper ways having to do with balancing the short term and long term, internal and external considerations, understanding and reconciling the interests of various business units, geographies, and functions, all while setting a clear direction for the business and managing relationships among people.

It takes keen mental ability and seasoned judgment to be a leader at the highest levels, the kind our best leaders have acquired through a lifetime of experiences and learning. But such judgment doesn't have to take a lifetime to acquire. We know such learning can be accelerated when we see a Jeff Immelt rising to be CEO of GE at age forty-four (he was one of Welch's long shots) or Michael Dell successfully leading a thriving PC business while still in his twenties. Given true leadership potential and the right experiences, a person's judgment can improve faster than you think.

This is good news for companies that want to select as their CEO someone as young as forty-five and no older than about fifty. Although it may be controversial to aim for a CEO in a specific age bracket, many companies realize that whereas the people running the company will grow older, the company itself must grow younger to successfully adapt to changing conditions, especially as the pace of change accelerates. Younger people tend to drive change rather than simply react to it. They are more likely to be on the offensive and don't have to be prodded to move forward.

The argument against someone rising to the top at a young age is that he or she won't have the depth of experience of someone older. But that is precisely the deficiency that the Apprenticeship Model is designed to overcome. It identifies leaders who are capable of exceptionally fast growth and gives them jobs where many things are unfamiliar and many more variables must be considered. Those who figure out how to deal with the ambiguity develop the mental framework and confidence to tackle a job with even greater complexity. When they practice several such rounds repeatedly, their knowledge gets deeply etched and takes the form of instincts and judgment. Leaders are put into those bigger jobs as soon as, or even a little before, they are ready for them.

With a cadre of leaders given precisely the kinds of experiences they need to expand through the Apprenticeship Model, the company can expect to have two or three viable candidates to be CEO when the succession decision is imminent. Naturally there is no guarantee any candidate will succeed in the job, no matter how impeccable the preparation. The odds increase greatly when leaders get the right opportunities and feedback, when the board is involved early and gets to know the candidates well, and when the process for choosing the next CEO is rigorous.

Why the Apprenticeship Model Works

Before you decide whether to take on such an ambitious undertaking, you should be sure you understand crucial differences between the Apprenticeship Model and existing approaches to leadership development. These differences are not merely mechanical but stem from different premises about what leadership capability is and how it is developed. Understanding the model's intellectual foundation might help you appreciate its value.

Concentric learning is a key concept in the Apprenticeship Model. Think of a high-potential leader's career progression as concentric circles of expanding scope and complexity, with the innermost circle being the person's fundamental, or core, capabilities in her first management job. If the next job involves greater scope and complexity and the leader has the talent to rise to the challenge, she will figure out how to apply the core capabilities to the new situation. Her capabilities will expand, and she will then be ready for even greater scope and complexity. This is the phenomenon I call concentric learning, and it is the goal of leadership development in the Apprenticeship Model (see Figure 2.2 for an illustration).

Figure 2.2 Leadership Growth Through Concentric Learning

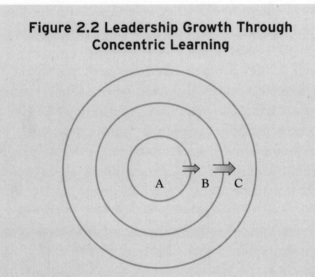

Leaders expand their capabilities through deliberate practice of a core skill in increasingly complex situations. Each new use strengthens the existing core and allows the leader to use it innovatively. Here's how a leader might develop his social acumen:

A. In an early job, the leader selects good people and gets them working well as a team.

B. In the next job, the leader influences and directs people who don't report to him, such as a cross-functional team or a group of suppliers.

C. Now the leader is running a global business and building teams of people from diverse cultures, with which he has no previous experience. He refines his instincts about people and deepens his understanding of group dynamics. He is now a good judge of diverse people and a keen diagnostician of complex group dynamics.

Deliberate practice is another key concept, one that goes hand in hand with concentric learning. We are all familiar with the term *practice* and usually associate it with athletics and the arts. How do you get to Carnegie Hall? Practice, practice, practice. But you don't become the first violin by mere repetition. High performance in leadership, as in athletics, the arts, and many other human endeavors, is the result of *deliberate practice over an extended period*—that is, practice that is repetitive and effortful, combined with real-time constructive and specific feedback and a willingness to take corrective actions. Deliberate practice—in short, practice combined with feedback and self-correction—is how business leaders refine their abilities and judgment. It is propelled by a person's drive and tenacity to grow and improve, even if the person is not conscious of it.

I picked up the term *deliberate practice* from K. Anders Ericsson, now of Florida State University. Ericsson has been researching the benefits of an individual's prolonged efforts to improve in music and sports and has authored or coauthored several articles on his research findings (see, for example, "The Role of Deliberate Practice in the Acquisition of Expert Performance," by K. Anders Ericsson, Ralf Th. Krampe, and Clemens Tesch-Römer, *Psychological Review*, 1993, vol. 100). I have taken an interest in his work because I found that it exactly matched the conclusions I'd drawn in my four decades of observing how leaders develop.

Deliberate practice works because it actually changes the way the brain searches for and processes information, etching pathways that make certain responses automatic and instinctive. It underlies the superb judgment successful leaders demonstrate. It is linked with concentric learning because leaders who deliberately practice their core skills may at some point find new ways to do them. They reinvent their mental framework or methodology. They innovate. Suddenly, whole new dimensions are built into their mental processes, and their core capabilities expand tremendously.

Some accomplished leaders have done this kind of deliberate practice as a matter of course and experienced tremendous leaps in concentric learning. It is well known that Jack Welch, the former CEO and chair of General Electric, was a superb coach and mentor to the leaders who reported to him and contributed greatly to their development and the success of their business units and functions. I observed him and GE over many years and can attest that he was constantly practicing and improving his management skills almost without thinking about it. When it came to making judgments about people, for instance, Welch seems to have internalized some of the most critical skills as a teenager when he was playing hockey. A highly competitive person, Welch realized early on that to win consistently at hockey, he had to recruit to his team superior players. Only if he had the most talented goalies and forwards would his team have a chance to win regularly. But expert players weren't enough. They also needed to work together as a highly synchronized team.

To lead that team, Welch had to get know his players well, both to realize their inherent abilities and to provide feedback and ideas to make them better. Helping individuals grow and work well together were core skills that he developed in himself by practicing them repeatedly throughout his career. When he assumed his first leadership job in GE's plastics division, he began to develop his team and conduct regular discussions about the business. He did the requisite reviews of his direct reports according to GE's buttoned-down formal methodology. But he also wanted a more informal way to work with people, so he started to end meetings early and would take the group to a bar, where they talked and argued until 10 or 11 P.M. He used those opportunities to get to know his people better, building bonds, getting more information, probing deeper, offering feedback, and evaluating each of them as individuals and as members of his team. He was assessing people's personalities and capabilities and, importantly, their grasp of the business. Here he began to develop another core skill: the ability to cut through to the guts of the business. He admits to making misjudgments of people early on, and most likely he misjudged the business issues at times as well. But he was always motivated to improve, and as he continued that practice of assessing people and the business, his judgment got better on both fronts.

As Welch rose higher and higher in GE's ranks, taking on more responsibility and dealing with increasingly complex businesses and situations that he knew nothing about, he relentlessly continued to practice the same kind of approach in which he engaged with people and got them talking directly and informally about the issues at hand. The whole time, he was accumulating insights and knowledge about the people and the business. He was practicing his ability to cut through to the core of the person to figure out what the person could be best at, to discover any flaw in that person's thinking, and to precisely understand and diagnose the business. As he sharpened his ability to analyze diverse businesses, he also found ways to translate that ability into results by improving the performance of each of the leaders who reported to him.

Welch applied his mental process in a rigorous, disciplined way in each quarterly operating review, quarterly budget review, twice-a-year strategy session, and talent session for each of his fifteen direct reports. Somewhere along the line, he came up with a way to make his coaching even more effective: after each review, and sometimes in between, he sent each leader a handwritten letter reinforcing the issues and action items that had emerged. Multiply the many reviews conducted each year times fifteen executives over twenty years, and it's easy to see how Welch would become a master at knowing the right questions to ask and drilling to the right issues. He also honed his personality traits through that deliberate practice—for instance, he built his confidence to question and challenge even extraordinarily high-performing leaders. As he practiced writing his feedback notes, he continued to innovate, coming up with better questions to ask and more insights in linking business and people issues.

Welch had the raw talent for business leadership and an incredible drive to continually learn, but it was his deliberate practice that allowed the concentric learning to take place and made him the quintessential business leader of our time. Until the day he left GE, he continued the practice of reviewing every business and manager at least five times a year. Still today, in his work with private equity firm Clayton Dubilier, he hones his skills by applying them to an even wider array of businesses. When it comes to pinpointing the strengths and blind spots of individual leaders, he is astonishingly precise.

The thinking behind the Apprenticeship Model, then, is to give each leader job assignments that allow concentric learning to occur through a combination of deliberate practice and testing in situations requiring the leader to grow. The sequence, timing, and content of those jobs are crucial. Leaders enhance their deliberate practice when they receive feedback that is specific and constructive and in real time, and that is why their bosses should provide it as they observe leaders practicing their core capabilities. The role of bosses as mentors is key to leaders' deliberate practice and concentric learning.

Chapter 3

HOW TO RECOGNIZE LEADERSHIP POTENTIAL

The Apprenticeship Model depends on spotting leadership talent early and correctly. As in sports, even the best coach can't build a championship team if he picks the wrong players to begin with. I start this chapter with a close look at Colgate-Palmolive, a company that's held its own for many years against powerhouse rivals Procter & Gamble and Unilever. Colgate's secret weapon is the depth of its leadership, all the way to the top; the company never even missed a beat when longtime CEO Reuben Mark announced in 2006 that insider Ian Cook would succeed him. Colgate's talent machine works in part because the company excels at identifying the specific talents of each potential leader early in the person's career.

As senior vice president for global human resources, Daniel Marsili is the trustee of their talent machine, which at any given moment is working closely with about 500 or so people among Colgate's 36,000 worldwide employees who have been identified as "global high potentials." The identification process is global because Colgate recognizes that talent is everywhere. It starts early because Colgate also recognizes that the earlier it pinpoints people who exhibit extraordinary skills, the better it can assign jobs to develop the broad-based global business skills Colgate needs in its future leaders, including a CEO.

"If you don't start early, you lose critical time to develop people broadly, and not just in their functional area of expertise," says Marsili. "You may have an expert at delivering a P&L [profit and loss] but who doesn't understand some of the company's broader

41

strategic aspects. The key for senior leaders is to have the balance of skills as well as the understanding of when and how to apply them."

Colgate's leadership identification and development process takes place at three levels: local, regional, and global. *Local talent* may be someone who is relatively early in his or her career but who can make it to the level of reporting directly to a general manager in a subsidiary, for example. *Regional talent* is someone with more experience, capable of going beyond a subsidiary to responsible positions in regions like Asia or Latin America. The *global talent* pool is at the core of Colgate's long-term succession planning. This is the group being groomed and tested to become the company's senior leaders for the next twenty years. These people will almost certainly enjoy successful careers at Colgate if they track well, continuously learn and change, and stay flexible in their career aspirations. Colgate's leaders are selected on strict criteria. No matter their country of citizenship, fluency in English is a given, as is an undergraduate degree from a respected university. Most have advanced degrees. Specific competencies for different functions or areas of the company also are required for the global talent development pool.

The real selection begins with a focus on several qualities of leadership. The first is how well the person demonstrates a set of leadership competencies that are more or less common to any company, such as people and communication skills. "We clearly want to ensure that we have people who have a unique ability to communicate effectively, and by that I mean all aspects of communications," says Marsili. "They need to be able to communicate their vision, but they also have to be good listeners, constructive and articulate and able to influence others. They are able to adapt to fast-changing business conditions and pull their teams together to focus and align them against the two or three really key things that drive the business. They're the folks who you would walk through fire for."

The second quality is how well the person operates within and sets an example of Colgate's unique culture and value system. Leaders are identified based on their ability to clearly articulate a vision, set priorities, motivate people, pull together and focus their teams, and perhaps most of all, celebrate people's individual and team successes. All of that falls under the principles of valuing people, operating with personal integrity, and managing with respect.

The ability to produce results is obviously critical, but Colgate also pays attention to *how* those results are achieved. As leaders progress and Colgate continues to evaluate their potential, results are viewed in the context of business conditions: A leader who can minimize losses in a bad economy or manage through a tough business issue, perhaps by mobilizing certain resources, is as highly regarded as someone else who hits a target under good economic and business conditions.

Leaders identified as global high potentials are also judged on how well they understand the breadth of the business beyond their functional expertise and can discern the significant differences among markets, especially between ones in the developed world and in less developed regions.

Identification begins at the lowest levels of the company. Each subsidiary's managers around the world nominate people designated as high potential using the criteria senior management has clearly conveyed. Local general managers decide which nominees get on a preliminary list that is sent to the division headquarters. At that level, the division functional heads—marketing, human resources, and sales, for example—review the list along with the division president. They can either add or subtract names from the original submissions. The resulting list moves up to the global level where functional heads once again review it and make adjustments. That list then goes to the chief operating officer, chief executive officer, and other senior leaders to make the final decision, subject to an ongoing dialogue through both formal and informal channels that gives everyone who participated in the nominating process a chance to articulate their support for an individual.

This list of five hundred or so global leaders is "like any other list of investment opportunities," says Marsili. "If you are going to support a brand, you have to invest wisely. It's the same with people. Great companies support all their brands and, likewise, support all their people. But some special investment is required with brands to become blockbusters and similarly with some people who may have the potential to become the next generation of senior leaders."

That doesn't mean that a candidate on the list stays there indefinitely. "We do the same process every year," Marsili explains. "The lists change because, as you would expect, as they encounter increasing complexity, some people come off, and others show unique talent and are added. Obviously, at higher levels, the list is smaller." The list also reflects the evolution of the company. A salesperson designated high potential ten years ago had to sell to a wide variety of accounts. To do that, he or she needed great interpersonal skills and excellent product knowledge. Today a salesperson deals with massive consolidated buying groups that have the most modern inventory and purchasing technology. Under those circumstances, a salesperson who aspires to be a leader must understand every nuance of the information technology system for his account as well as logistics, financial margins, promotional spending, gross-to-net spending, and merchandising. To get to a senior level, a salesperson, regardless of which market he or she starts in, will have to get exposure to all that and be tested to see if he or she can go further.

One of the few derailers is that as people rise in the ranks, they can lose their ability to adapt to rapidly changing conditions. Other high potentials may decide that they don't want to make the big changes in locale required by Colgate's global presence and take themselves out of the high-potential pool. And as they rise higher in Colgate's ranks, subtler judgments are made about them. As you would expect, senior leaders need much more sophistication in reading a situation, working with internal systems, and dealing with all the complexity associated with doing these things. Some leaders reach a point where it's hard for them to pick up the skills to represent the company and make good decisions in different countries and regions. Those abilities are imperative for senior leaders in a company as decentralized as Colgate.

Practical realities also shrink the list of leaders with high potential. Changing family patterns can present particularly challenging circumstances in managing a global pool of talent. These days, both men and women have careers and do the parenting. The challenge, according to Marsili, is to have really good mechanisms to ensure that no mind is wasted and to stay current on people's abilities, aspirations, limitations, and capability, whether they're twenty-five years old or approaching retirement.

That's why Colgate's talent identification process allows for the discovery or rediscovery of high-potential leaders at different ages. Marsili says that while it may be unrealistic to think that someone whose talent is discovered in his forties could have a shot at becoming a CEO, the company "can do some pretty interesting accelerations of people," particularly those who did well early in their career, then scaled back for whatever reason and want to resume that career, especially in staff functions.

What we learn from Colgate is to identify high-potential leaders early, treat them as such, and be consistent and clear about what you consider to be the earmarks of leadership potential. Once identified as having high potential, leaders get a great deal of attention, but they also undergo scrutiny to see how, and if, they are progressing, and people move on and off the list accordingly.

Focusing on the Essentials

Do you think you know a leader when you see one? Most companies have the wrong notion of what a leader really is and does. Yet all the development efforts in the world can't deepen the leadership pool if they're focused on the wrong people to begin with.

The brilliant strategist, the creative genius, the financial engineer, and other bright people command attention and respect, and rightfully so. People recognize such individuals' knowledge and intelligence, respect their opinions and ideas, and appear willing to follow them. Combine that great mental ability with a strong work ethic and drive to achieve, and no wonder people are impressed. Unaware of their own shortcomings and driven to succeed, these experts push for leadership jobs at higher and higher levels, persuading—sometimes even intimidating—their bosses to promote them. But many lack essential leadership traits. Although they may succeed for a while when put in charge of other people, without a natural ability to lead, they are unlikely to ever succeed as CEOs or high-level leaders outside their domains of expertise.

What does a natural leader look like at the age of twenty-five or thirty? The usual attempts to answer that question take the form of laundry lists of personal qualities. These are important, but on their own they can be misleading, especially because the same wonderful personal qualities can be found in political leaders, spiritual leaders, and leaders in sports, many of whom don't have an ounce of talent for business. Besides, many personal traits and capabilities associated with leadership in the past are insufficient today. You have to go beyond the list of personal traits you're looking for to include other indications that a person can succeed in leading a business function, business unit, or whole company in the emerging business context.

One way to think about the raw talent or inner engine of a business leader is to think of two strands of a helix: people acumen (the ability to harness people's energy) and business acumen (understanding the essence of how a business makes money). The beginnings of these strands are pretty much in place in individuals by the time they reach their twenties. After that, we can test someone's people acumen and business acumen and give them opportunities to expand them. But we don't yet know how to implant them in mature people who lack them entirely. That's why spotting these strands, however undeveloped they may be, should be central to any effort to identify leadership potential. People who lack them are unlikely to ever reach the highest leadership levels, no matter how many other leadership traits they possess. Only when people acumen and business acumen are present in some degree should personal traits come into play.

It's fruitless to argue whether those talents and personal traits are born or made. We know they begin to manifest themselves early in life and are firmly in place in some people by the time they join the workforce. Some of those qualities may be latent and come to the surface only later under certain conditions—such as when a person who is not the official leader suddenly takes charge of a crisis. But it is unlikely you can implant them into a mature person without inherent leadership abilities to make him or her a leader.

People Acumen

Leadership is predicated on the ability to mobilize others to accomplish a vision, a goal, or a task. Leaders can't do everything; they get other people to do things through managing. They increase their capacity—the ability to get more done—through delegation combined with a methodology for ensuring follow-through. They set expectations, get the best people to do what needs to be done, and oversee the relationships among them to ensure that destructive or self-interested behaviors don't subvert the group's common purpose.

You know you've discovered a leader with people acumen when you see evidence that the person selects the right people and motivates them, gets them working well as a team, and is able to diagnose and fix problems in coordination and social relationships among groups of people.

Real leaders, I have found, exhibit an enthusiasm for selecting people who are better than they are—whether or not they have worked with them before—and then using those subordinates to lift the organization and themselves to new levels of accomplishment. They motivate their people and develop them as conditions change, retaining those who advance the business and having the courage to deselect with dignity those who don't. Such leaders show a repeated pattern of accurately identifying other leaders' talents, helping them flourish, or easing them into other jobs where their talents fit better. You can often identify a true leader because the people working under that person are of high caliber, are energized, and have a natural affinity for the leader and want to see him or her succeed.

Leaders with people acumen get the most out of their people by setting clear goals, then giving feedback and coaching judiciously to help achieve them. Most use some kind of performance indicators (the term I use is *key performance indicators*, or KPIs) that not only measure progress in quantitative terms but also influence behaviors. A KPI may be as simple as the percentage of customer calls answered in the first minute or may be as broad as corporate profitability measured against competitors. They watch for problems that might get in the way of achieving the KPIs and don't hesitate to give people unvarnished feedback. They are keen judges of when someone is not up to the task and don't back off from making the hard decision to replace him. Many people who think they're leaders are terribly uncomfortable and indecisive in the realm of personalities, even when they have the insight into who and what needs coaching. Some have a deep-rooted need to be liked that compromises their judgments of people.

Anyone can improve his or her ability to select and develop people's talents, but other aspects of people acumen are hard to teach. Leaders with people acumen have good instincts to anticipate problems among individuals who must work together and to get them resolved. They size up the group dynamics and pinpoint simmering conflicts, then draw them to the surface to unblock the group's progress. They intervene when they detect behavior that disrupts the working of the group. These leaders are fearless where many people are unconsciously concerned that if they try to change the group dynamics, they'll be cut apart or ignored and lose face.

Social acumen also manifests itself in network building. Leaders who possess it are not loners or bookworms. They have an innate desire to work with diverse people and naturally cultivate a broad range of social networks that permeate the company, including subordinates, peers, and superiors. As these leaders develop their social acumen, their networks often extend beyond the business to include customers, suppliers, regulators, politicians, and various interest groups. The relationships tend to be durable because they are built on trust, and that trust allows information to flow both ways, exposing the leader to new ideas and different ways to see things. The social networks also allow him or her to energize and synchronize people's energy and actions and to do a better job managing a crisis than would otherwise be the case.

Business Acumen

Every successful businessperson, whether a street vendor or the CEO of a global empire, has a basic understanding of how the business makes money. The essence of making money is managing the profit and loss (P&L) as well as the balance sheet of a business in the context of the external world. Let there be no mistake, profit *and* loss is a much broader concept than profit *or* loss. Managing the profit and loss within a business requires that a person take in myriad factors and pieces of information—much of which is incomplete or distorted— that contribute to either a profit or a loss, connect those various conflicting things, and make the trade-offs among them with the clear goal of making money and generating cash on a sustained basis. The leader must also know how profits and losses interact with the company's balance sheet, which indicates the health of the company.

This cognitive ability to conceptualize the working of the business is present and highly developed in every successful CEO I have known. It is the CEO nucleus defined in Chapter Two: "the intuitive ability to comprehend the total picture of a business and how it makes money in the language of a street vendor."

We can't expect a thirty-year-old leader to have the business acumen of a forty-five-year-old, but an intuitive feel for business is evident at an early age if we bother to look for it. These are the people who intuitively understand the connections between customers, profits, money they borrow, and money they take in. This business acumen is evident even in the simplest contexts, such as that of a small shop with a well-defined customer base and a handful of competitors. You see it in shopkeepers who mark the prices down in the right increments at the right time, buy the right merchandise, and create the right shopping experience, constantly making adjustments to keep the cash flowing. They have a knack for making the right trade-offs and decisions, and the business prospers.

You also can see it in some leaders at the lowest organizational levels and in the earliest stages of their careers in a big company. They have a sense of how their company makes money, what it really offers customers, and how it compares with the competition. Given the chance to run even a tiny P&L center, they have the ability to weigh multiple factors, from changes in the external environment to internal constraints, in deciding how to position the business and expand its moneymaking. They understand the relationships between the variables, do the mental processing to determine which are most important, and make decisions that deliver clear, measurable business results.

As the scope of a leader's job increases, so do the number of variables and the uncertainty about them. The complexity grows exponentially. The leader needs greater mental breadth and depth to make the connections between the complexities of the outside world and the intricacies of moneymaking. She also needs incisiveness to cut through that complexity to the shopkeeper fundamentals. When leaders are unable to make good decisions, or any decisions at all, it may be that their business acumen is not expanding. They cannot be considered to have CEO potential. A sales manager who becomes the executive vice president of marketing and product development may face the problem of identifying the need for innovative products that will satisfy new customer needs. He has to balance the risks of developing those new products against the business's growth, all of which requires a broader scope of thinking and acting. If he can't do it, that's a sign that his business acumen will not develop fast enough for him to become a successful CEO of a major company. Leaders who continue to develop their business acumen, or CEO nucleus, expand their capability, or their ability to add more value per increment of time by taking on more complexity, ambiguity, and uncertainty.

The search for business acumen will help keep other traits and skills in perspective. For instance, great communication skills help leaders motivate people, implement a strategy, and win over customers, investors, and the public. But business acumen defines the *substance* of the message being communicated. Some young leaders can excite and lead their group to deliver on stretch goals, but can they define where the group is going? Are they decisive, and can they sort through multiple alternatives to find the right pathway forward? Can they use their business acumen to choose the right goals and KPIs? With practice, any leader can improve, but some leaders are naturally better at it.

Other Indicators of Leadership Potential

In my many years of observing leaders, I have noticed a number of other signs that a person has high potential for corporate leadership. A wide cognitive "bandwidth"—the capacity and inclination to see things in a broader context—is an earmark of a CEO who anticipates how changes in the external environment will affect the business or of a marketing vice president who sees how marketing relates to overall company direction. Leaders aren't born with the phenomenal breadth and scope of thinking that characterizes successful leaders of big companies, but those with a drive to constantly search for more information and see things from a broader view have the potential for it. Some young leaders exhibit a conceptual ability to rise above the details, to see a broader context than their peers, and to place themselves and their immediate accomplishments within that broader context.

Look for actions that reveal such thinking. I know of one instance in which a high-potential executive was asked to add two more divisions to her portfolio of responsibilities. She demurred, pointing out to her boss that while she would welcome the additional responsibilities, the two divisions would be better placed with one of her colleagues because they were complementary to businesses already under him. Her willingness to put the company's interests above her own ego reflected not just a great personality trait but also her ability to think strategically and from the viewpoint of the overall business.

Drive and aggression are common criteria for identifying leaders and are conveniently easy to observe even in very young people. What boss wouldn't notice the young sales rep who pushes hard to win more and more business and outshines his seasoned peers in hitting targets? But a rep who does her job to a tee and also seems to have a handle on what her sales manager does—and even what the regional sales director does—is demonstrating something more than drive: a desire and ability to see the bigger picture.

Leaders must also be able to make sense of all they take in and set a clear course of action. After gathering information from multiple sources and shaping several alternatives, they have to be able to sort out what is important, make a decision, and act on it. Even at lower levels, information is often muddled and the right path is often unclear, but leaders with high potential find clarity and act decisively despite the uncertainty and ambiguity that stymies others. They take disparate facts and observations and connect the dots to create a clear view of what they think is likely to happen before it actually does. Because they see the hazy outlines of change coming before others do, they put their businesses on the offensive.

Most high-potential leaders will show an uncommon ability to analyze and synthesize large amounts of data and make a decision based not only on the data but also on intuition. They have a way of clearing the fog. They frequently use the "80-20 rule," which states that 20 percent of factors account for 80 percent of value. They sift, sort, and select information based not only on its content but also on its source. They think in second, third, and fourth orders of consequence, are extremely clear about goals and constraints, develop alternative paths, and have a backup plan in the event a decision proves wrong.

Business leaders make judgment calls on a daily basis as they balance the inherent tensions between the short term versus the long term, between shareholders and customers and employees and external constituencies, and between opportunities and aspirations versus real-world realities and constraints. Some people are simply not decisive or tough enough to lead the business. They let opportunities slip away, powerful personalities dominate, and other people set the course. These people are not leaders, regardless of the depth of their thinking.

Another sure sign of leadership potential, and one that is especially important in today's environment of tumultuous change, is the leader's passionate quest to continually learn and grow. High potentials seize the opportunity to take "stretch" assignments that tax their abilities precisely because they are stimulated by the challenge and the opportunity to increase their knowledge base about the business, people, and the external world. They are intellectually honest and have the self-confidence to acknowledge when they don't have the answers, knowing they can find them. They are dissatisfied with incremental progress and the status quo. They continually search for new ideas and different ways of seeing things. This insatiable thirst for learning tends to make them more contemporary than their bosses, more aware of leading-edge technologies and trends.

Don't forget to look at integrity and drive to screen out those who fall short. Leaders must tell the truth at all times fearlessly and without weighing the consequences. When confronted with a moral or legal quandary, they must always choose the ethical course of action. Leaders must also radiate a sense of urgency. In the course of being tested, over the years a high-potential individual will be given increasingly broad and difficult jobs. Without relentless drive and near-total immersion, he will find it difficult to maintain the endurance necessary to master tasks.

Diversity and DNA

What I just described are criteria that apply to leaders in any business, which companies will want to select and sharpen to their liking. They will also want to go beyond those general criteria to particular qualities, skills, and even attitudes relevant to their business. Doing so will ensure that they meet their leadership needs and give them an edge by differentiating themselves from other companies. The challenge is to define what your company considers important in its leaders and to ensure the criteria are up-to-date and anticipatory of where the company will be in the near and distant future.

History shows us that too many companies narrowed their definitions of a leader and failed to update them, leaving them short of leaders for changing conditions. In the 1970s and 1980s, for example, companies like IBM, Xerox, and General Motors had what appeared to be excellent leadership development programs that were regarded as benchmarks within their industries. Yet, none produced the kind of CEOs that were most needed by those companies. Something was wrong in their leadership development framework. It may have looked good in theory—they all had the formats and templates and went through the proper motions—but in practice, those programs failed to take into account the rapid changes occurring in the context of the business.

Xerox and GM failed to produce leaders capable of recognizing the scope of the rising challenge from Japan; they were all internally focused. IBM failed to develop leaders who could make a successful transition to the new realities of competitors who were selling mainframes for 35 percent less, the emergence of distributed computing, and the growth of lucrative business opportunities in software and services. Its leaders rose through the company based on deep but narrow functional expertise rather than business acumen, which was needed to reposition the business. The companies that have done well at developing their own executive talent, among them General Electric, Johnson & Johnson, and Colgate-Palmolive, anticipated change and selected leaders who were prepared to shape it and deal with it. In 1995 GE was already thinking about the leaders it would need in India and China in 2005.

Every company's leadership pool has a "DNA," or commonality in the basic makeup of its leaders. Companies in the same industry will likely have similarities in their DNA, but there will also be some differences. The best companies are conscious of their DNA, not only to ensure that they choose leaders who mesh with it but also to shape it and intentionally differentiate it from the competition. They design into their leadership selection criteria precisely the characteristics, skills, and capabilities they want emphasized. They change the corporate DNA over time, usually in an evolutionary way, though some companies have had successful DNA revolutions.

Jeff Immelt has been gradually changing the DNA of GE since he succeeded Jack Welch as CEO. In GE over the past twenty years before Immelt, the DNA produced general management talent through P&L experience and multi-industry experience. A high-potential young executive coming into GE could clearly feel that he could move from one industry to another because GE operated in at least eleven industries. The key under Welch was the absolutely unmistakable ability to execute in processes, productivity, and cost reduction. In the late 1980s, GE began to globalize and as a result of that began to make a shift. It still emphasized general management, productivity, and process, but it also pushed potential leaders to stretch themselves to work in a global position. Nevertheless, the fundamental DNA of operational discipline and excellent execution remained intact.

Since Immelt took over as CEO, he has been shifting the DNA, evolving it to meet new challenges. In the past, much of GE's leadership pool arose through the internal audit function among people who had business acumen and who could dissect the numbers and determine cause and effect. If they had the requisite people skills and were identified early, they had a good chance of becoming a general manager. Now the world is changing, and Immelt sees that top-line growth is essential. He has set a goal of delivering organic growth of 8 percent per annum, roughly twice the rate of the world's growth in gross domestic product. The goal recognizes that the center of gravity of economic growth is shifting, and the strategy to accomplish that growth calls for 60 percent of it to come from emerging markets like China, Brazil, and India, where rapid infrastructure growth plays to many of GE's strengths. Clearly leadership development at GE for the foreseeable future will be focused on identifying and growing a pool of talent, much of it outside the United States, that can see the worldwide picture, not just a regional picture, and help the company grow.

The implementation of the leadership part of GE's strategy can be seen at GE's John F. Welch Leadership Center at Crotonville, New York, where half the most recent class came from emerging nations. Although the company still focuses on developing general managers strong in operational and execution discipline, it is putting much more emphasis on non-U.S. experience and on the ability to find opportunities for top-line growth through technology and marketing expertise. Immelt has in fact laid out explicit criteria for the "growth leaders" GE is looking for, and the criteria are driving the identification of leaders at all levels.

GE Leadership Criteria

- Create an external focus that defines success in market terms
- Be clear thinkers who can simplify strategy into specific actions, make decisions, and communicate priorities
- Have imagination and courage to take risks on people and ideas
- Energize teams through inclusiveness and connection with people, building both loyalty and commitment
- Develop expertise in a function or domain, using depth as a source of confidence to drive change

Where to Find High-Potential Leaders

The search for high-potential leaders begins with recruitment, but it certainly doesn't end there. The longer a leader's tenure, the more information you have about that person and the more accurate your assessment of leadership potential will be. Avoiding common errors—identifying as leaders people who really aren't, or missing great leaders in your midst—means continually revisiting the talent pool, removing those whose talents didn't materialize, and allowing for the possibility of adding leaders whose talents have suddenly come to light. Most high-potential leaders should be identified early on, either in the recruitment phase or shortly after. Hiring people with a master's degree in business administration (MBAs) from Ivy League schools is no guarantee of leadership ability. Certainly the best graduates demonstrate fast thinking, conceptual agility, facility with numbers, and many other skills that are valuable in business. Without the raw talent for leadership, they should be considered high-potential *individual* contributors, not high-potential leaders. They are certainly important and worth recruiting, but don't depend on them to be your future CEOs.

On the other hand, people with leadership skills who lack analytical skills can go further. They can tap others to do the analytical work they need. In today's tougher environment, you have to focus your time and energy on sorting through the MBAs who have the raw material, the natural talent to be a leader, from those who have other intellectual gifts. Recruiters on college and business school circuits should be attuned to incipient signs of leadership. Those signs can be as obvious as whether the recruit quarterbacked his college football team or was president of the senior class or as subtle as whether the individual can sway a group discussion and make clear decisions.

Grade point average and peer recognition awards are less telling. Leaders will seldom have the highest grades, and the people who are top-notch experts often are happiest operating within their domain. Look at how this works in the finance function. Most people in finance come through the precise and narrow path of accounting. The leaders who eventually become chief financial officers (CFOs) are among the relatively few accountants who learn through experience to deal with ideas and ambiguity, sharpen their judgment, and link their discipline to the fundamentals of the business. Only a small percentage of CFOs go on to be CEOs. These are the ones who exhibit the necessary breadth of thinking and people skills.

Recruiting potential leaders from other companies is important to keep the talent pool diverse and flexible. Although an influx of outside talent can disrupt an organization's cohesiveness, the value of new ways of thinking makes it worthwhile to bring in outsiders as leaders at several levels below the CEO. If the idea is to keep the leadership talent pool diverse and refreshed, companies must be sure to assess a person's leadership potential and not just domain expertise.

Any leader with a year or more experience in a corporate environment will have begun to demonstrate leadership qualities that reveal her likely potential. A set of criteria or questions can guide discussions with aspiring leaders, whether inside or outside of the company, and help separate the wheat from the chaff. (See the box, "How to Spot a Leader," for some suggestions.)

The military is another source of leadership talent. Its leadership training is second to none. People who have been through it and seem to have a natural interest in business can be a good bet. Interviews can further test the extent of their business orientation.

The recruitment of leaders is in and of itself a test of any leader. Like everything else, experience in recruiting—both the successes and failures—provides an opportunity to learn and improve the skill. Those who lack experience at it will at first rely heavily on explicit guidelines, but over time, with sufficient practice, recognizing a high-potential leader among the pack should become more instinctual. After practicing and self-correcting, you'll get to the

How to Spot a Leader

Many people who think they know how to recognize a leader focus on highly visible attributes and skills, such as analytical brilliance, charisma, the ability to make great presentations, and the drive to succeed. These are fine things to have, but they aren't sure signs of leadership ability. Look instead for the actions, decisions, and behaviors that reveal true leadership potential:

1. What is the person's ambition? Is it clearly for a leadership role, or is it oriented more toward making an individual contribution?

2. Does she take pride in accomplishing goals on the basis of her own ability, or does she talk about bringing together and motivating others to achieve those goals?

3. Does the person seem curious about subjects outside her area of expertise?

4. Does she have a grasp of the business and basics of moneymaking?

5. Can the person articulate clearly the requirements for doing her boss's job well? Her boss's boss's job?

6. How does the person ensure that she is continually learning?

7. How well does she deliver results, and what is extraordinary about the results?

8. Does this person have an incessant drive to shape the external environment and make progress?

9. Does she like to work with diverse, high-caliber people, or does she bring along with her to a new job the people she is comfortable with and who are loyal to her?

10. How driven and passionate is she about leading? Is it just talk, or is it realistic?

11. Is the person dealing with increasingly complex and uncertain situations and using the occasional failure as an opportunity to learn?

12. Is there clear evidence that this person has a methodology to continue to build new skills and hone her personality traits to achieve her dream of what she wants to become?

point where you know a high-potential leader when you see one. As leaders at every level develop their skill in identifying and recruiting leaders, the organization overall gets better at it, and the quality of the leadership talent pool improves.

Don't Leave Leadership to Chance

I can't begin to count how many leaders have told me they were just plain lucky that someone recognized their leadership talent early in their career. Some describe the pain of being forced to leave a company that didn't see it in them and then the joy of landing in a company that did. How many potential leaders pass their careers in relative obscurity because no one recognized their leadership abilities, and how many companies missed out on their talents?

GE almost missed Jack Welch. He was working as an engineer in GE's plastics division when a superior recognized his leadership potential and gave him a job that required him to learn marketing. He took the reins between his teeth and never looked back. He knew he had the talent and was absolutely driven to succeed, so he pressed hard to get a P&L job. For whatever reason, he was denied it at GE, so he decided to find it at some other company. He submitted his resignation and even attended a going-away party thrown for him. But then a person higher in the organization realized that GE couldn't afford to be losing people like Welch. He persuaded the impatient young executive to stay with the company and soon found him the kind of job he needed. From then on, every job Welch took had P&L responsibility with increasing complexity and ambiguity that tested him and allowed him to improve his leadership abilities.

Finding leaders can't be left to chance or to mechanical processes that create false confidence that the company is developing the leaders and succession candidates it needs. Every company has leadership talent. To build great leaders at all levels, companies must first learn how to find them. Of course, that's just the start. The next chapter provides concrete guidance for helping them develop.

Chapter 4

CUSTOMIZING LEADERS' GROWTH PATHS

The Apprenticeship Model requires companies to be creative in custom designing talent tracks that take each leader wherever he or she needs to go to unleash his or her talent quickly. You are not only handpicking your leaders, you're also handpicking their jobs so that each assignment provides the right kind of developmental challenge for that leader to grow as fast as possible. Bosses must be willing to take some calculated risks by giving leaders jobs that stretch them.

That's just what Doug did. Watching Amanda in product development meetings and other venues, he saw that she had a firm grasp of how to create engineering solutions for complicated products. But he also saw the glimmer of something rare in an engineer: business acumen. Amanda could see how engineering decisions would affect marketing, sales, and profits at her own company and at the customer's. When an opening occurred in Europe for a regional marketing executive, Doug decided to take a chance and put her in the job.

Would this young engineer be up to the job of learning a new field, and in a foreign environment? "We had a candid conversation," Doug said later. "I told her she and I were both taking a big risk, but that if she felt confident that she could adapt to very stressful circumstances, then we ought to try it." Amanda took a few days to think about it and asked Doug if she could talk to some of the other executives about what would be involved. The questions she asked were smart and analytical and helped reassure Doug that he wasn't going to have a disaster.

That was three years ago. Today Doug's experiment with Amanda is counted as a great success. Although Amanda felt some anxiety at first, she approached the new job with energy and fresh ideas that weren't just extensions of what her predecessor had been doing or repeating what made her successful as an engineer. She learned about her biggest European customers and bridged a gap between technology and marketing by getting people from those functions to talk with each other and to meet jointly with customers. She turned around the mind-set of European product development teams from "excellent technology will sell" to "customer needs will drive the choice of technology" and got them focused on developing products for predetermined price and cost points. Reorienting the entrenched culture tested Amanda's leadership capabilities, and she passed with flying colors. The evidence was concrete: her huge changes in the European organization produced increased revenues, margins, and market share.

It was a big break for Amanda to be able to expand beyond her functional expertise early in her career. And the company now has a leader who has been tested, has demonstrated tremendous growth, and is ready for an even bigger assignment. But had she been in a typical company, it wouldn't have happened.

Traditional approaches to succession and leadership development don't allow leaders to move far beyond what people know they can do. They put leaders on the same well-trod career paths, moving them up incrementally in vertical lines. For example, Amanda would have advanced a notch within the engineering function. Such incremental steps fall far short of providing the mental challenges a leader needs to be prepared for success at the highest levels. They also drive talented, ambitious people to turn elsewhere, often outside the company, for their next big challenge. Would a leader like Steve Jobs have risen to the top through the traditional career paths typical of most companies? More likely, he would have quit in frustration early on.

The result of customizing talent tracks is not only a greater number of leaders prepared to lead at high levels but also wider diversity among them. When the time comes to choose a new CEO—or a leader at any other level, for that matter—a company using this approach will have a wider and deeper pool of candidates from which to choose, giving the organization tremendous strength and flexibility.

Development Paths That Allow for Leaps

High-potential leaders often grow in spurts, and their talent tracks must allow for that kind of expansion. They should be given jobs that are several notches up in scope and complexity and that force them to exercise the mental skills to find a clear path through it. When a marketing vice president becomes a business unit manager with profit-and-loss (P&L) responsibility for the first time, for example, suddenly he has to see the outside world from a different point of view, deal with ambiguity and uncertainty, and open his mind to figure out new ways to achieve success. He has to be able to diagnose the situation he finds himself in, build new relationships, and find new sources of information. If he rises to the challenge, he gains not only new skills and perspective but also the self-confidence to deal with unknown situations and, as a result, an appetite for taking them on. The experience hones his personal attributes, expands his capability and capacity, and prepares him for bigger, more complex challenges.

I've observed such growth spurts in many successful high-level leaders. They explain why some leaders are successful at a relatively early age. Jack Welch and Jeff Immelt at General Electric, Andy Grove of Intel, Reuben Mark of Colgate-Palmolive, Michael Dell of Dell Computer, Andrea Jung of Avon, and Ivan Seidenberg of Verizon immediately come to mind as people who expanded the depth and breadth of their understanding of business and improved their judgment quickly. (See Figure 4.1.)

Richard Carrión, the CEO of Banco Popular, Puerto Rico's largest commercial and consumer bank, is another excellent example of how a talented person can grow in leaps to become an

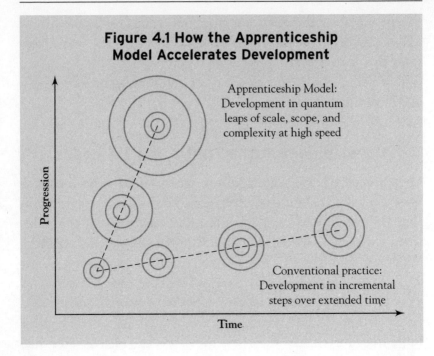

Figure 4.1 How the Apprenticeship Model Accelerates Development

Apprenticeship Model: Development in quantum leaps of scale, scope, and complexity at high speed

Conventional practice: Development in incremental steps over extended time

Progression

Time

effective leader. Although he and Banco Popular were not explicitly using a leadership development process as formal as the Apprenticeship Model, the learning experiences he talks about are precisely the kinds of challenges that rising young leaders need to engage.

Carrión's family had run the bank for generations, and although he didn't plan to make his career in the family business, the apple didn't fall far from the tree. He earned a master's degree studying finance, accounting, and information systems; took a summer job at the bank; and wound up staying for more than thirty years. He started by using his technical skills to reorganize operational areas of the bank. Over time, as he was given more and more responsibility, he found that he was supervising individuals and groups of people who knew more about certain topics than he did. "That was the first critical leap for me in becoming a leader," he says. "I wasn't the guy who knew the most about a subject, but I was the one who had responsibility for making the decisions. I had to learn to ask the right questions, to recognize talent, and to delegate authority to that talent. It was a tough first lesson." It was a lesson he learned well.

Carrión's second leap came in 1987, when he oversaw a major restructuring and change process designed to shake the successful bank out of a growing complacency. It was a leadership challenge to conceive of the restructuring and figure out how to implement the change so it would take hold. When people resisted, Carrión realized that his success depended on a capability he had not developed: persuasion. He would have to convince employees that it was the right thing to do.

"It was difficult to do because I thought I was a lousy communicator in large groups, and to some extent I still do feel that way," he says. "I went out and sold the restructuring through a series of regional meetings in which I put some very hard numbers on the wall. I said 'this is where we're going to be in five years, and these are the things that you have to focus on.'"

The restructuring led Banco Popular to make a large acquisition in 1989 to strengthen its market position in a consolidating industry, a move that tested Carrión's political and communication skills externally. "I thought the acquisition was just an economic transaction that brings together shareholders of two companies who are going to benefit," he recalls. "But I learned it was a lot more complex than that. There was quite a bit of uncertainty among the public and the regulators and even about whether it would be approved. I had to learn external communication skills to convince people that this move would create a stronger institution and enable us to compete better."

The merger was finally approved but immediately spawned yet another test. "It was a huge learning experience to do the work to put the two organizations together and meld them into one," Carrión says. He learned by doing it.

"I was forced to think of new ways to put two cultures together. There were instances when I had to choose an executive from the acquired bank and say goodbye to a good-performing person in my original bank. Those decisions tested my values and self-confidence to focus on the right thing. Streamlining the merged business meant reconciling two paths for decision making into one organizational structure. Accountability and roles had to be assigned quickly and thoughtfully while managing the egos to retain the best talent. Meanwhile, I had to keep the company running day to day. It was like changing the tires on a moving vehicle."

Carrión is an incessant learner who distilled from his experience a mental template and guiding principles that he would use repeatedly thereafter. "We did another acquisition a few years later," he said, "and it was so smooth that it was almost second nature. So you do get better at it." Since then, he has aggressively expanded the bank's footprint into the mainland United States, largely through a string of successful acquisitions.

Not every person would have learned the lessons Carrión learned or mastered the new situations as quickly, but each new challenge tested Carrión in a different way. Some of his natural abilities were underdeveloped but emerged and improved in the heat of the situation. The diversity of the experiences broadened his scope and capacity as a leader. Today he is a highly valued member of the Puerto Rico business community and a board member of Verizon, which itself was built largely through two megamergers and now gets the benefit of his well-developed business judgment.

When is a leap too great? When it puts the leader or the business at undue risk. Companies must be sure they can withstand the consequences if the leader doesn't rise to the challenge. Sound judgment is required. I have recently seen several corporations try to broaden their succession pool by putting leaders in jobs they were nowhere near ready for at crucial junctures for the business. In one case, the company's chief planning officer—I'll call him Frank— had caught the board's attention as a possible successor to the CEO because he was extremely bright, knew the ins and outs of the business better than anyone except the incumbent CEO, and was imaginative and creative. He had built his career in a staff position and would need testing in a line job first, so they gave him the job of running the North American division. The company was in dire financial straits and facing tough price competition. The division, its crown jewel, needed a turnaround. Let's see if Frank can do it, the CEO and board thought.

But Frank had never supervised more than a hundred people and had neither the mental framework nor specific skills to lead such a large organization. He had not developed the instincts to select or coach people in operations and could not establish credibility with them. He failed to mobilize the organization and made some poor decisions. He was eventually taken out of his job, as was the CEO, but the damage was done. Within two years, the North American division took a huge dive. Its market share went from 20 percent to 15 percent, cash flow went negative, and the company's bond ratings declined to junk. Competitors gained several years. It was a leap all right, but it also was the wrong job at the wrong time for an untested leader.

Defining the Growth Path

The search for the right job for each leader turns conventional practice on its head. Most companies try to find the people for the jobs. In the Apprenticeship Model, the job is chosen, redesigned, or even created specifically for each leader. The content of the jobs you give your leaders is the crucial difference in whether you're developing them or just moving them around. You have to be clear about what you are trying to discover and build in a person, which means you have to thoroughly understand what's required of high-level leaders and what an individual leader's talent is, then be creative in defining the appropriate learning in the next job.

Two people in similar jobs in the same company could well have different development paths and next steps. That was the case for Wayne and Elaine, both of whom were global brand managers who performed well in their jobs. Wayne's bosses noticed that even in his staff job, he acted like a line manager, building strong relationships with the various country managers and taking strong ownership for their success. Although he was young, he seemed to have the seeds to one day be a CEO. So the company moved Wayne quickly into a P&L job as head of one of the smaller, simpler country operations where his challenge was to ramp up performance and change the business model. Next, they moved him to their division in Germany, which was not only bigger but also had more diverse customer segments and external constituencies. Besides handling the increased complexity, he would have to shake up an entrenched culture. If Wayne succeeded in that role, as his bosses believed he would, the plan was to have him make a big jump and run all of the European operation.

Wayne's colleague, Elaine, had done well, too, in her staff job as a global brand manager. After several years, some leaders thought it was time to move her to run a country-level P&L, as Wayne would do. On further thought, however, her bosses saw Wayne and Elaine differently. They realized that whereas Elaine had been successful in working with research and development (R&D) and had good marketing skills, she had been too literal in following the marketing models and had stepped into some unnecessary conflicts. They had doubts that she had the collaborative skills or the business acumen to succeed as a country manager. In the past, the company might have put her in a country manager job anyway to "round her out," but this time, they chose a talent track where she could excel, giving her bigger challenges within the marketing function but not P&L responsibility.

Each job should allow the leader to expand existing capabilities while testing his ability to acquire new ones or to glean more insight into the leader's talent or personal traits. For example, does he have the resilience and psychological reserves to tolerate uncertainty and ambiguity? Put him in charge of an organization in crisis (not the crown jewel), where morale is down, critical people are leaving, the competition is intense, and cash is being depleted rapidly.

Building the CEO nucleus is a must. Leaders should start with a core understanding of money making, then develop that capability by moving from simple situations to those that are more complex. Dealing with greater complexity means having to consider more variables—such as volatility in foreign exchange; combinations of political, business, and financial risks; and fast-moving technologies—and the myriad interrelationships among them. Leaders need to make four or five leaps in complexity to be ready to be CEO, starting with P&L and balance sheet responsibility in simple situations and moving to highly complex ones. By repeating the fundamentals but with more complexity, leaders develop an intuitive feel for moneymaking. This is the concept of concentric learning introduced in Chapter Two. Finding the opportunities for concentric learning is the centerpiece for accelerating leaders' growth.

P&L responsibility early on is crucial for leaders to develop their CEO nucleus. Any staff people who have leadership potential should be sure to get it. Some staff people rise high in their organizations through a functional silo, and only when they're near the top do they catch the eye of the CEO or board. By then it's almost too late to put the person in contention for a senior leadership position or the CEO job because she won't have built her CEO nucleus. Instincts and judgment don't materialize overnight; they develop over time through the school of hard knocks and come from concentric learning. This is why so few CEO candidates emerge from information technology, human resources (HR), finance, legal, and strategic planning. People in staff jobs who have leadership potential should be put into line jobs no later than five years after they begin their careers. Even if they return to their functions later in their career, they will be better at their jobs if they've had P&L experience.

Leaders should start early to expand their social acumen as well by applying it in larger, more complex organizations. Making judgments on people outside their domain, managing cross-functional teams, and motivating people in different cultures are all opportunities for leaders to build their core capabilities. Potential leaders in staff jobs are accustomed to making recommendations in their specialties, but to build their social acumen, they need the chance to create a methodology and acquire the skills to get them executed.

They may also need to practice being decisive in selecting the right path forward.

Being able to handle the myriad challenges of the global environment is an imperative for many leaders today, so leaders must expand themselves beyond a single culture. It's not good enough to have direct reports in other countries. Running a business in China from New York is a completely different experience from living in China while running the business. The leader must be immersed in that milieu to get the experience necessary to deal with different cultures and different constituencies, such as government agencies, nongovernmental organizations, and the special interest groups that are becoming increasingly influential in corporate affairs.

Having defined the desired experiential learning for their leaders, companies should find creative ways to provide it. P&L experience, for example, can take many forms, such as placing the individuals in a marketing position charged with creating a P&L by customer, brand, or product. Consumer goods companies like Procter & Gamble often use this method with great success. The person doesn't have all the authority but is accountable for the profitability and health of the brand. She must therefore track and try to influence the multiple and interconnected variables that affect it, from inventory levels, product quality, pricing, and consumer acceptance to demographics, industry trends, and alignment with major customers like Wal-Mart. A leader in that kind of job also gets practice in working collaboratively with people outside her expertise. Manufacturing companies often assign P&L to plants and plant managers, who become familiar with costs, inventories, and pricing. As soon as possible, those manufacturing leaders with high potential should be moved into broader jobs that also require learning about markets, growth, and competition.

The best move may not be up but sideways to a job outside the leader's functional discipline at the same hierarchical level or perhaps at a nominal step down. Whatever the specifics, the horizontal move has to stretch the leader. It can't be a matter of rotating her through business functions or geographies or having her apply the exact same set of skills—for example, cost cutting—repeatedly in different settings. One leader grew the top line in every job he held by merely raising prices each time. He never stayed long enough to suffer any negative consequences or to expand beyond his existing skill. His limited growth caught up with him at higher levels, at which point his career abruptly ended.

The goal in a horizontal move is not so much for the leader to learn the technical content of a new discipline or to become conversant about it but rather to integrate it with the old one so that she gains a better view of the business as a whole. The challenge is to look at the disciplines from a different angle, learning the viewpoints of people in both. The leader must not make the mistake of getting co-opted by the new discipline, coming to see the business from a different but equally narrow perspective. If a leader in finance goes to a manufacturing operation, for example, his task is not to follow the plant manager around blindly, learning every facet of how to run the plant. Instead, he needs to look for ways to blend his financial expertise with what he is learning about manufacturing. New insights and innovations often emerge as the leader synthesizes his learning from two different areas with the total business as the frame of reference. For example, he might see in the manufacturing operation an area in which increased efficiency would have a big effect on cash yet not increase the chance of running out of inventory at peak demand. That kind of breakthrough thinking can transform both functions.

Not every leap in learning requires a new job. Some functionally organized companies provide important experiences by putting potential leaders on task forces. WellPoint, Inc., one of the largest administrators of health plans in the United States with some $50 billion in annual revenue, tests young high-potential executives in their regular jobs by assigning them to projects that are part of the company's ambitious "2010 Plan." Those projects tackle a range of real company issues, some of which involve the P&L. The leaders assigned to them have mentors, and an HR person administers the program. Randy Brown, executive vice president and chief human resources officer, says there are two powerful benefits for the company: "We get the projects done, and we get to observe the capacities of these young leaders," who range in age from their late twenties to their early forties.

Last year I attended an all-day board meeting of Genpact, a company that manages outsourced business processes; the agenda items ranged from financial performance and future financial expectations to acquisitions, succession issues, strategic issues, and ideas for developing talent and enlarging HR capabilities in the fast-growing company. What struck me was that the CEO of the private equity firm that owned it brought with him four young high-potential leaders. He explained that he made a habit of it because he knew those leaders would grow by being exposed to the range of issues and rigor of the discussion. He had no doubt that by having them analyze the issues ahead of time, attend the meetings and occasionally participate in them, the young leaders would absorb the nuances, judgments, and incisive questions that seasoned leaders exhibited in those sessions.

Sometimes the job itself changes, creating opportunity for growth. When a large manufacturing company changed its strategy from being a low-cost producer of what had become commodity goods to providing value-based solutions for its industrial customers, the chief operating officer (COO) faced an enormous new challenge. He still had to pay attention to productivity and cost management, but he also needed to understand customers better and anticipate their needs. He had to make a shift in his own mental orientation and then ensure that other people were shifting theirs. Salespeople would no longer be order takers but a source of information and ideas. They would need to work closely with production to know what solutions were possible and at what cost. Transforming the relationship between marketing and production was a huge challenge for a leader who had succeeded by driving hard on cost, cost, cost. In addition, he would have to create new ways to gauge sales expertise, an area where he lacked experience. His ability to make the shift was pivotal to the company and to his own chances to be in the pool of CEO candidates. The CEO, after thinking hard about both the man and the demands of the job, judged that the COO could make the leap. That decision appears to have been correct; the COO is indeed growing into the job, shifting his mind-set and operationalizing a stronger focus on customers and a new approach to sales.

Clearing the Path

No matter how well you plan for your promising leaders, you're bound to run into a variety of organizational and practical difficulties. You'll have to be creative in finding ways to keep them from blocking the leaders' progress.

Rarely can a company put its finger on the perfect job to provide the desired learning. If a high-potential leader needs a challenge that doesn't exist, you have to be willing to shift responsibilities and perhaps even organizational structures, say by combining several regions into one to test a leader's bandwidth, using creativity and resolve to keep leaders progressing.

One of your most challenging tasks may be to unblock a job held by a leader who has done her job well but is no longer growing. These situations must be handled carefully because every leader must be valued and treated with dignity. In a well-developed Apprenticeship Model, ongoing assessments and feedback will help people be realistic about their prospects. But leaders are still likely to feel devalued, and perhaps angry and resentful, if you're asking them to leave a job to make room for a rising leader. Few moments are more difficult than when you're sitting face-to-face having those discussions. You can ease the disruption by making sure they, too, get jobs in which they can discover new talents and expand. There are many instances in which a leader is rejuvenated by being moved to a new situation. In any case, high-potential leaders warrant extraordinary consideration because the future of the company depends on them.

You may encounter resistance from bosses of high potentials, and you have to understand its root. I know one company that weighs how well the leader and the boss will get along and complement each other before placing a leader in a job. But some bosses resist having a rising leader assigned to them because they don't want to take a risk on someone whose skills and capacities are untested, or they may be afraid of being outshined by an ambitious and aggressive person.

An opposite but equally common problem is the leader who tries to prevent a transfer because she doesn't want to give up a star performer. She may, for example, try to hide him, not giving him visibility with the higher-ups. This is the same behavior you see in a leader who tries to hoard the cash his business unit is generating to keep it from being allocated elsewhere.

Resistance can't be tolerated. The deployment and development of leadership talent needs to be a corporate priority that every boss understands and acts on. It is a core value. Anyone who doesn't subscribe to it doesn't belong in a boss's job. If you're not seeing an increasing number of bosses taking a proactive approach to finding and asking for leaders or if they seem to be holding back the leaders who report to them, something is wrong in your implementation. An open job-posting system, in which all leadership jobs are transparent companywide, can expose leaders who repeatedly have trouble filling jobs, perhaps because they stifle the people who work for them.

Senior managers must demonstrate their commitment to developing leaders by driving and rewarding new attitudes and behaviors toward it. They can't assume people will get it right away. They have to repeatedly impress on people the importance of leadership development to the ongoing prosperity of the business.

Sometimes obstacles to growth originate with the very people you want to advance. You have to tackle these case by case. An increasingly common problem is the rising leader who doesn't want to make the next big leap because it means relocating the family. A leader may be deeply focused on her career path, but her spouse may have different priorities. Careers of their own, community ties, and concerns about uprooting the kids: these may outweigh any putative gain in family income or prestige down the road.

Some locations are simply unattractive, and even ambitious leaders eager to test themselves in new circumstances may be reluctant to take assignments in locations considered "hard duty." Can you find an equally challenging job where the person is now living or a similar one in a more attractive location? If you find too many people in the leadership pool resisting a move to a specific location, perhaps the business, not the people, needs to make a move. I know of several companies that have done this.

Horizontal moves can be troubling to leaders who are looking to go up, not sideways. Both the company and the individual should understand the value of a carefully thought-out horizontal move. There will be need for more and more of them as globalization accelerates and more companies move toward matrix structures.

The truth is that some obstacles in the talent track cannot be overcome. For instance, one company planned a move for Jon, the leader who was favored to succeed the CEO. Jon had done well running their European operation, and now the board and CEO wanted him to run the larger North American division as the final step in preparation for the top job. But Jon didn't want the job or the move. He knew North America was riddled with political problems, and his family was deeply rooted in their European home. The CEO and board then had a tough issue to contend with. Jon's job was a crucial testing ground for other CEO candidates, and because Jon was taking himself out of the running, his job had to be unblocked. Jon ultimately left the company to become a CEO elsewhere in Europe, and the company gave another promising CEO candidate the chance to test herself by running the European division.

Freedom to Fail

Whatever the specifics of the talent tracks you design, they have to give your developing leaders the chance to make their own success—or not. The learning experience won't be complete, and the test won't be valid, if a leader isn't free to fail. The environment you put leaders in must meet three criteria:

1. *The freedom to set ambitious targets for themselves that redefine their job.* Leaders don't merely accept the status quo; they want to reframe a job in the context of the future they anticipate and intend to shape. They set personal and business targets calibrated to their vision of the opportunities that lie ahead. A boss needs to understand and accept all this but at the same time can't allow a rising young leader to reach so far as to upend his own well-crafted plans. Together they must explore alternatives to arrive at a "win-win" solution.

2. *The latitude to lead the team they inherit in whatever way best suits them, making their own judgments about people and motivating them to achieve goals.* They must also be free to upgrade the team, without causing unnecessary disruptions and breaks in continuity, as quickly as they can.

3. *The freedom to determine how best to balance the business's short-term and long-term needs.* Everyone is expected to hit the numbers for the current period. But setting those numbers should be a collaborative process that takes into account a rising leader's ideas about investments needed immediately to set the stage for better long-term performance. The leader will make those choices based on her judgments about the broader context. Even if the context goes a different way—say, the economy unexpectedly weakens—the leader will gain important experience figuring out how to meet the short-term challenge in light of it.

Some people will be uneasy giving unproven leaders so much latitude, but when companies are rigorous in identifying leadership potential and in thinking through how a leader will likely perform in a prospective job, more often than not the learning happens and the leader succeeds. Nonetheless, giving leaders the freedom to fail means some of them indeed will. You should view those failures as an opportunity to improve your talent-tracking skill. Get to the causes: Were there mistakes in matching the leader to the opportunity? Perhaps a leader had exhibited a knack for pushing growth yet was placed in a cost-cutting job. Or a person who disliked foreign cultures was expected to adapt to one. Maybe the company gave a leader too big a jump because of the person's own desire and drive. High-potential leaders continually push for bigger challenges; a constant pursuit of personal growth and new challenges is itself an earmark of high-potential leadership. It is important to distinguish, though, whether the leader's drive is resulting in job hopping or real learning and growth.

Failure is not necessarily the end of a leader's talent track. Many people who fail in one job flourish when they are reassigned to another that better fits their talents and skills. Each job reveals more about the leader, and the Apprenticeship Model taps that learning to recalibrate the person, provide more effective coaching, and decide what the best next job will be. The leader's new boss must then get to work to help the leader develop in it. The boss's role as mentor is the subject of the next chapter.

Chapter 5

THE CRUCIAL ROLE OF BOSSES

A leader in the Apprenticeship Model has not done his job if he delivers only the numbers. He needs to deliver future leaders as well. Every boss is a mentor and coach who invests energy and care in helping develop the high-potential leaders who report to him.

Why should this be part of bosses' jobs? Because they're the people best situated to observe rising leaders in action, ask questions, make suggestions, and keep them focused on the right things. Giving feedback and coaching becomes part of the boss's routine work, like managing the budget or getting product out the door. Every interaction between the boss and the leader becomes an occasion to aid the leader's deliberate practice and growth.

Bosses are also the eyes and ears of the company, gathering information about the leader, to answer a crucial question: What learning is in fact taking place? When you put a high-potential leader in a job that's a big leap, you hope to see a huge expansion as the leader takes hold of the unfamiliar situation. But not every leader rises to the challenge. Other talents might emerge instead. The boss is on the front line, determining the nature and extent of growth and searching for clues about the leader's natural abilities.

Periodically the boss and others should take the time to pool their observations of the leader's *actions*, *decisions*, and *behavior*. From that, they can crystallize where each leader is on his or her growth trajectory. This kind of recalibration of leaders winnows and refreshes the leadership pool with up-to-date facts about how each person is progressing. It is an important check against moving leaders too fast before they've mastered the current job and have built a solid base for the next big leap. At the same time, it's a chance to brainstorm about how to unleash a leader's true potential, which will link to designing the leader's talent track.

Being at the center of leadership development is an entirely new role for traditional bosses. Even if they think they should be developing new leaders, most don't. They're not expected to do it, and they don't necessarily know how. Senior management and human resources (HR) need to clarify the importance and create a mechanism to recalibrate leadership talent. The typical annual performance review won't do the job. Performance reviews are basically a time to look at past performance and determine compensation. They look in the rearview mirror at what the leader has accomplished, usually in terms of quantitative measures. The leaders conducting them rarely go beyond the mechanics of the process to probe the circumstance under which the person met, or failed to meet, her targets or what she actually did to achieve them. Virtually never do performance evaluations define the leader's natural talent.

With continuous feedback and periodic recalibration, leaders develop faster and can move ahead but never before the required learning has taken place.

Bosses as Mentors

The best bosses are advisers and teachers who adhere to the old Chinese proverb: Give a man a fish, and you feed him for a day. Teach a man to fish, and you feed him for a lifetime. As mentors, they help high-potential leaders unleash their talents in the current job and raise their sights. When mentor-bosses spot an obstacle or an opportunity for further growth, they can give the leader feedback right away. Such informal real-time coaching can achieve more than any formal performance appraisal, especially when it repetitively reinforces a single element that the leader needs to focus on. Some bosses will complain at first that taking on this role takes too much time. But it's more a matter of discipline than time. GE's Jeff

Immelt says he pores over the list of 175 top leaders at his company each and every day, thinking about where they fit, what they can do, and who needs to go into another job soon. As observing and providing feedback becomes part of the boss's everyday routine, it gets to be second nature. And bosses who are good at it attract better people, thereby expanding their own capacity. (See the box, "What Makes a Good Boss-Mentor.")

The Apprenticeship Model puts leaders in particular jobs for clear and specific learning purposes. Bosses have to watch the things

What Makes a Good Boss-Mentor

- Identifies leaders and helps them grow as a central mission of his job, maybe even of his life; continually searches for ways to help the leader grow

- Makes insightful observations of the person, pauses periodically to reflect on them, and accurately identifies the person's talents, whether or not they are fully developed

- Pinpoints one or two things that would accelerate the leader's growth if they were to improve

- Is intellectually honest, courageous, and respectful in giving feedback that is direct and timely

- Asks incisive questions that expand the leader's perspectives or range of alternatives and deepens the leader's grasp of the issues at hand

- Follows through to help a leader succeed even when he or she no longer works for him; takes great pride in a leader's success

the leader is expected to learn while keeping their perceptual lenses wide open to see the leader as a whole person and someone with perhaps some talents and personal traits that are as yet undiscovered. The idea is to dig for insights into what one or two items could propel the leader if he or she improved. Those are the things the leader should practice and the boss should coach on. Many bosses will want to jump to personality traits, which outside coaches usually focus on. But whereas a leader's behavior and attitudes are important, developing business and social acumen is usually more critical.

Bosses know that even the simplest P&L and balance sheet experience can provide insights and knowledge that become the foundation for business acumen. They should watch the many facets of business acumen, including the ability to see and seize opportunities, reduce complexity, detect when the old ways of making money have become obsolete, figure out a new moneymaking model, evaluate risk, balance the long-term and short–term issues, and understand the relationships among various financial measures. How good is the leader's judgment in these areas?

Bosses can observe aspects of a leader's social acumen almost every day. How well does the leader motivate people, develop new leaders, and build a team of people who report directly to her? Specific skills that contribute to a leader's social acumen include things like pinpointing people's talents, communicating, getting conflicts resolved, creating mechanisms for the free flow of information, diagnosing problems in interrelationships, and putting the right people in the right jobs, all of which require intuition combined with decisiveness.

Bosses should observe whether these capabilities are expanding and whether leaders' judgment is in fact improving, bearing in mind that personality traits and psychology might factor in. How well they motivate people is a good example. Leaders have to be able to get others to collaborate and improve performance, which may require them to acquire new skills. Designing incentives is one such skill and a particularly important one for a sales force. Selecting or designing the performance metrics is another skill, and setting goals is yet another. A leader has to combine those skills to design an incentive program that works. It's fine to set goals that stretch a team's capabilities but wrong to set impossible goals. It's fine to reward superb performance but wrong to also reward mediocre performance. Did the program achieve the desired behavior? Results will be visible fairly quickly.

Bosses should see if the leader can influence behavior in other ways, such as bringing conflicts to the surface and getting them resolved constructively. Does the leader do it in a way that builds trust and respect? Does she correctly spot the people or issues that undermine the working of a group? Does she provide the specific focused feedback to those who cause discord behind the scenes? Maybe the leader is having trouble diagnosing where the conflicts lie, standing up to high-ego team members, or identifying the right people to bring together.

Focusing on business and social acumen doesn't mean ignoring behavior, attitudes, emotions, and values. Some people think these are intangibles, but they aren't. They are observable hard facts. They don't change from day to day, and they drive a leader's actions and decisions. Bosses should watch how the leader's skills combine and how her personality traits and psychology are affecting them. For example, how is her eternal optimism affecting her sales forecasts? If the forecasts are unrealistically high, inventory will pile up, and prices may have to be discounted, which could tarnish the brand and shave margins. How is her risk profile affecting her appetite to pursue new opportunities? It will give clues about the leader's bias that could someday change the fate of the company. At one point Yahoo had the chance to buy Google for a few billion dollars, but the leaders at Yahoo didn't make the bet. It was a fate-changing decision, no doubt affected by the leaders' appetite for risk as well as their strategic skills.

If judgment is weak in a particular area, bosses as mentors should try to get to the cause and unblock it. Say the leader keeps missing on resource allocation, overfunding a slow-growing product line while underfunding a more promising one. Is it because he's wowed by the young hotshot or perhaps cowed by the consistently high-performing person who's making the request? Pull him aside and make him aware of the pattern. A high-potential leader will gird his confidence and sharpen his thinking around resource allocation and will likely apply that learning to other areas of his decision making as well. His capabilities will greatly expand.

Is she making the right trade-offs in setting goals? Is she selecting the right people and motivating them to increase their capacity? What is getting in her way? These are the kinds of questions bosses should consider. (For more, see the box, "What to Coach On.")

What to Coach On

The following questions give a sense of how broad the spectrum of coaching might be. In their role as mentor-coach, bosses must be selective, specific, and consistent in the feedback they give. It is best to sustain a focus on one or two items.

1. Is the person decisive, willing to shake up and upgrade the business and people to change direction and set and accomplish new goals?

2. Does the person push himself and others to innovate to keep the unit on the cutting edge?

3. How well and often does the person deal with external relationships?

4. How well does the person manage her time by determining the correct priorities and delegating and assigning the best people to new initiatives?

5. How well does the person build cohesive teams, both within and outside his hierarchical power? How well does he facilitate group dialogue?

6. How perceptive is the individual in detecting new areas and approaches to growth?

7. How well does the person drill down deeply into issues, simplify complexity, and see an emerging picture? Is the person detail oriented enough? Too much so?

8. How good is the person at identifying and developing new leaders?

9. Does the person play the hand that is dealt him to maximum advantage, or does he whine about the resources—financial, human, and otherwise—he is given or about the circumstances confronting him, such as extreme competitive challenges or declining markets?

10. Does the person demonstrate emotional extremes that are detrimental to others?

11. Does she exhibit signs of arrogance, which might suggest an unwillingness to learn? Does she make psychological contracts with people that inhibit her ability to build the strongest possible team?

12. Does there appear to be a mismatch between the person's potential and his aspirations?

13. Does she have the tenacity to stick with a person who is growing? Is she able to discriminate between sticking with a good person who will benefit from development and sticking with someone who will continue to be a burden?

14. How does the person deal with setbacks and disappointments?

15. Is the leader more interested in being respected or in being liked?

(Continued)

16. Is the person inclined toward doing something himself rather than getting it done? Does he delegate enough or too much?

17. Does the leader exhibit the emotional strength to bring conflicts to the surface in a group setting and the skills to oversee the resolution of a conflict?

18. Does the leader demonstrate an inclusive mind-set that naturally encourages teamwork and collaboration across hierarchical boundaries?

19. What are the leader's "hot buttons"—the issues that unconsciously trigger a negative response or loss of temper that creates toxicity in the social dynamics?

20. What is the person's appetite for risk? Is he realistic?

Sometimes bosses can help leaders dissolve psychological and cognitive blockages by drawing attention to them. Other times, a blockage is organizational, and the boss may have to intervene. If, for instance, the leader cannot take hold of his job because a stubborn person in another function is hoarding information and the leader's diplomatic skills aren't working, the boss should step in. Sometimes resources have to be reallocated by people several levels higher than the leader can influence. The leaders themselves should try to work around such problems, but sometimes they can't.

The point is to keep leaders focused on the one or two things they must deliberately practice so that their personal traits get honed and their skills get tested and hopefully expanded. This is the process of concentric learning that I introduced in Chapter Two. The more frequent the practice, the more the capabilities expand and the deeper the core capability becomes etched. The more *deliberate* the practice—that is, the more focused the feedback and self-correction that occurs—the better and faster the leader's judgment will improve.

Deliberate Feedback

When I was in Shanghai recently, I sat in when a business unit head made a presentation to his CEO about how to grow his business in China. He could barely contain his excitement as he laid out his vision for expansion. He had defined a huge opportunity by linking changing demographics with rising incomes among the middle class, which was prompting consumers to seek higher-quality merchandise. He tied all of that to a forecast of increased demand for the company's products and higher-priced, higher-value products the company could introduce. The CEO of the company listened intently and, when it was over, drew the presenter aside. He complimented the leader for his great presentation and hard work. Then he gave some valuable advice: "You used per capita income expressed in local currency in your presentation, but it would have been better if you had used income in terms of purchasing-power parity. That would change some of your projections about demand and call for more aggressive expansion of our business in China to seize the opportunity."

The CEO's comment was noteworthy in several ways. It was targeted, important, and timely, and it was delivered in a way that made it easy for the leader to accept. The CEO was being honest, candid, direct, and business minded. You could say that bit of feedback was deliberate: squarely aimed at developing the leader.

Bosses must tune in to the subtle clues that arise in daily work and connect the dots about a leader. Observing the leader in several settings, a boss might, for instance, notice a psychological bias toward people who are like-minded. An otherwise excellent leader might be completely unaware of this tendency. Once the boss points out the pattern, the leader might widen her lens and start seeking more diverse viewpoints or communication styles. The boss will likely have to repeat the feedback and watch to see if the advice is taking root.

When, for instance, Scott, a division president, kept missing target dates, Meg, the group executive he reported to, pondered why. She had noticed that Scott's engineering chief was not delivering and that Scott was failing to hold him accountable. Missed deadlines was one of the problems Scott had hoped to rectify when he'd hired the engineering chief eight months previously. Meg saw it as part of a pattern: Scott seemed predisposed to go easy on people he had hired. That tendency was compromising his judgment of people and his own performance. In discussions about the progress of engineering projects, Scott too readily accepted the engineering chief's excuses for delays. So Meg talked to Scott and suggested he probe more deeply. Scott did, and asking tougher questions, he came to see that the engineering chief didn't have a handle on what was going on in his department. He didn't delve into the details of the projects he was managing and therefore wasn't identifying and rectifying the bottlenecks. Scott reevaluated his engineering chief and concluded he was wrong for the job. Reflecting on the situation, Scott realized there was a bigger lesson, which he took to heart. He began to revisit his decisions about people more frequently, to seek a more balanced view of them, and to stay sharply focused on performance.

When feedback is deliberate, leaders sincerely appreciate it. In fact, they actively pursue it, and the whole relationship between the boss and her leaders becomes more open and trusting. Communication gets more honest and spontaneous, and the learning and self-correction happen faster. If the leader doesn't listen and adjust, he can no longer be considered to have high potential.

Deliberate feedback should also be a natural part of the monthly and quarterly operating and budget reviews bosses already conduct. Reviews are a terrific opportunity for bosses to take stock of leaders—not just whether they are hitting their targets but how well they are taking hold of their jobs and what they should focus on going forward. The boss should ask questions and get into specifics to know how things are progressing, why, and how the leader is handling situations as they arise—all crucial for execution. If, for example, a leader's sales target was $1 billion and he actually achieved $1.1 billion, the review needs to uncover why that happened. It could be something as simple as a strong market, but it could also be that the leader helped a regional sales manager to focus better on his customers' needs and to achieve sizable market share gains in his region. If a leader misses her target, is it a problem with the business or a problem with people? This is no place for psychological hesitation. Bosses must be decisive and confident as they delve in, even when the leader is highly capable and confident.

After the discussion, the boss should take the time to reflect on what was covered and draft a note. Jack Welch made a habit of doing this, and his notes were always personalized and handwritten. He added this feedback mechanism to his repertoire as he honed his skill in coaching and mentoring over the course of his long and illustrious career.

Letters should be short and sharply focused on a few things that are pivotal for the leader. The letter below, an abbreviated and slightly disguised version of one a boss sent following a global operating review, is an excellent case in point. Joan, the boss, made a practice of giving written feedback after every such review to reinforce what was going well, identify areas to improve, and ensure that her leaders had laser-sharp clarity about priorities. Effective reviews and feedback letters, she found, improved their performance—and her own.

She knew Max, a country manager reporting to her, had taken a big jump to this job. It was his first line job from a staff planning position. She wanted to let him know that she appreciated his superb diagnostic skills. But she also wanted to define areas where Max needed to improve to succeed in his current situation. He had to probe deeper to pinpoint the talents of his team members and better match them to the business's needs. His marketing person was good with channels but not strong on consumer insight at a time when consumer insight was crucial to the business. She left room for Max to come to that conclusion. She also posed a challenge to him: to demonstrate that he could make tough calls on people, especially when he had no domain knowledge.

Here's how Joan spelled it out:

Dear Max,

Your presentation convinced me that you have really taken hold of our deteriorating situation in India in the short six-month period you have been country manager. I was impressed by your grasp of the concrete and most relevant details of the causes for that deterioration:

The quality of the products is uneven because the training of factory supervisors and product installers got cut significantly to save costs.

Turnover of high-talent people has increased because we did not match the inflation in salaries and total compensation due to the general shortage of talent in India.

Our marketing campaigns have been inconsistent and erratic, causing market share loss and decline in free cash flow.

I am encouraged by your tenacity and determination to turn this around. Your proposed action items requiring more resources and investments will reduce profit targets for the next four quarters, but they are well reasoned. You will have to be vigilant to ensure those resources are correctly targeted.

For our next meeting in ninety days, I'd like you to focus on the following:

1. How are you building the leadership pipeline in view of the continued bidding war for talent in India?

2. How will your marketing campaigns distinguish you from your competition? What information will you be receiving from the ground to know that the market share gains will materialize?

3. I'd like to review with you the ten most critical people and jobs that will help you take this business from the level of disappointing performance toward one with excellent performance.

4. I like your benchmark data. I know it's difficult to get, and you did a good job. But we need more clarity on the real cause of the market share decline. It must be anchored in insights about consumers. Why did they not prefer our offerings compared with competitors'? It will be extremely useful for us to discuss this question at the next meeting.

5. I'm glad you brought your senior VP of marketing and other team members to the review. As you know from our discussion after the meeting, I have some real questions about the VP. He is aggressive and seems to be very good in dealing with the channels. He has good relationships with them and regards them as critical, as he should. What I'd like you to determine is, Does this person have the capability to get consumer insights? Can he use those to influence the channels and therefore the customers? As his boss and the leader, you will have to make this judgment. Let me know your evaluation.

I fully support what you're doing and focusing on, but for you to succeed, you really need to step up to improve your consumer insights. This may test your resolve as a leader. You have my confidence.

—Joan

Every up-and-coming leader benefits from deliberate feedback, but for high potentials, it is essential for maintaining their momentum. Once you understand that, it should be clear why bosses are the best people to provide it and why the outside coaches many companies use so often disappoint. They are brought in for their skills in the psychological and behavioral aspects of leadership, but they're not in a position to see the leader in action in a variety of situations and therefore have a limited base of observations to work with. They also don't know all the relevant business issues and rarely have the nose to sniff them out. Besides, behavior is easier to correct when the problem is addressed at the moment it surfaces or shortly afterward.

If outside coaches are used, they should have an ancillary role. They can be effective sounding boards for an individual facing a particular issue. A call to a coach can result in ways to resolve a problem or at least determine what the alternatives are. If, for example, a leader needs to talk about the best way to deliver bad news to a subordinate, the coach, who presumably has a great deal of experience and skill in asking questions to get a full picture of the situation, can help by giving the leader some options. The best way to use outside coaches is to involve them early in the leadership development process to help a person develop inherent strengths. The scope of their coaching should not exceed their expertise.

Keeping Track of a Leader's Growth

Giving feedback and coaching are ongoing, but every boss should have a routine to periodically take pause and consider the progress of each direct report. How is he coming along, and where can he go next? For some bosses, once a quarter is sufficient. Those who make a habit of it look forward to those moments, just as they eagerly track their quarterly numbers.

Organizations should help the boss with an annual "leadership recalibration session" that combines the observations and thinking of several people who know a leader and whose sole purpose is leadership development. This is in addition to performance evaluations and other kinds of numbers-driven assessments. Most people think evaluations based on numbers are the ultimate in objectivity, but numbers alone can be misleading. Evaluations that rely on them are often shallow and sometimes even dangerous when ethics and corporate culture are so important to the long-term health of a business. Delivering targeted results is important, but numerical measures on their own shed little light on what a leader has actually done; they completely disregard *cause and effect*. An improving economy can help even a mediocre manager hit an artificial target whereas a declining economy can prevent the best manager from achieving a numerical goal. The lists of leadership competencies some HR departments use to rate individuals are similarly inadequate. They seldom capture the nuances and all the critical ingredients of leadership and don't help companies detect the unique mix of capabilities and traits each leader has.

An annual leadership recalibration provides the opportunity to probe the capabilities the leader has demonstrated, what others are seeing in the person, and where he or she might go next. These sessions should be designed and conducted to allow all dimensions and nuances about the person to emerge. Then companies can be sure they know the quality of their leaders and can adjust their plans and expectations for each one. This is a way to correct misjudgments by the boss and prevent the wrong leaders from moving up the leadership trajectory.

General Electric and Colgate-Palmolive are among the few companies that have rigorous processes expressly for calibrating leaders' talents. When they look at a leader's performance, they consider all the factors contributing to and detracting from it. They read between the lines to figure out what makes the leader tick and think imaginatively about where he or she should go next. Some other companies have tried to emulate GE's lauded "Session C," the annual review process that powers GE's talent machine. Those attempts usually lack the depth and rigor GE and Colgate bring to the process and often fail to include anyone other than the boss.

Thomson Corporation, the Connecticut-based provider of information for professional services businesses, also has an annual calibration session much like GE's Session C in which it discusses leadership talent overall as well as specific leaders. The people discussions are linked to its strategic planning and budgeting processes throughout the year. In January, the senior executives confer to determine the corporate priorities for the year. Then in the spring, they review the strategy, focusing not on the numbers but on uncovering opportunities based on what's happening with markets, customers, and broader external trends. In the summer, the senior team looks at the organizational and leadership implications of where the company is heading, including discussions about specific high-potential leaders and direct reports. They tackle budgeting in the fall, based on previous discussions of strategic direction and planned organizational changes.

"Planning, budgeting, and people are all part of a single process now," says Jim Smith, executive vice president and chief operating officer of Thomson, and not just because they are designed to build on one another. As they are discussing a business item, an opportunity, or a performance issue, they automatically connect the business issues to people. If an initiative was handled well, for instance, Smith will ask, "Is it an individual or a team who's responsible?" If there is a new opportunity the company wants to pursue, he'll field suggestions for who might lead the effort to go after it. The insights inform decisions that may be made on the spot or become part of the evolving knowledge base about each leader.

Every session is an opportunity for the senior team to observe leaders in action. "Because of the way we have interactions, we get to see managers talking about strategy, working with others, talking about their people, laying out budgets, and doing actions plans," says Smith. "It isn't just one observation by one person, it's *multiple* observation points by *multiple* people. We get to judge people in various formats and see more people in more settings. We see who has a real commercial sense, who can see market discontinuities that can be exploited, and who knows how to make the money."

At the end of the session, the CEO, chief financial officer, chief operating officer, chief technical officer, and the head of HR talk about leaders. The chief technical officer is included because he is a great business unit manager as well as a great technologist. He and the chief operating officer work well together in assessing people who can straddle technology and marketing and sales. As these senior leaders integrate everything they've heard and compare their observations, they can determine who needs to make a move and who needs to be watched more closely. Reevaluating leaders is thus ongoing throughout the year.

Dialogue as the Principal Tool

The key to developing an accurate and nuanced calibration of a rising leader is periodic facilitated dialogue among several people who have observed the leader in action.

The fact is that people talk behind other people's backs all the time. The Apprenticeship Model elevates those conversations beyond gossip while allowing people to discuss each leader in everyday language unconstrained by the predefined competencies some companies use. The facilitator sets a tone of informality and candor, and the nuances naturally emerge. For instance, in discussion of one high-potential leader, a colleague of the leader's boss kept saying, "something about him doesn't sit right with me." The group kept talking to try to understand the discomfort, and it eventually came out that the leader had experienced a kind of mutiny among his direct reports early in his career. For that reason, he didn't trust people who weren't extremely loyal to him. No checklist would have unearthed that insight.

The beauty of this dialogue is that other people serve as a cross-check on the boss's perceptions, which might be biased by the closeness of the relationship. I have seen bosses defending their subordinates only to realize partway through the discussion that they really can't substantiate their view and that the truths emerging from the discussion are far more compelling than their individual opinion. I have also learned that any time several thoughtful people see a particular quality in another person, that quality is almost certainly a fact. But let me add that all observations must be illustrated through examples.

Dialogue works well as a tool because it captures the entirety of the person under discussion. It doesn't force people into pigeonholes. It weighs traditional performance measures against the leader's means of achieving them. Many important capabilities come to light amazingly fast in the course of a dialogue about a person, especially when the group digs for cause and effect. In one case I observed, it was known that the leader had made a timely and high-quality decision about which new market segments to enter, but discussion of her performance revealed that she had done so with a group of people she had no hierarchical power over. That is a noteworthy capability, and the discovery led to discussion of how her skill might be useful elsewhere in the organization.

Dialogue can also identify negative qualities better than a list of competencies. The boss may comment that his subordinate is aggressive, a broad thinker, and good at coaching his people but that he can be reckless. He might offer an example. If another person offers up a different example of recklessness, then it can be safely assumed that the person in question does in fact have this tendency. Recklessness may well be a fatal flaw in the context of the person's next job. It emerges readily and naturally from open discussion. What's more, dialogue can expose and develop the nuances that occur when traits and skills combine in a unique combination and allow people's tone of voice and body language to convey the strength of their opinions.

Further, dialogue helps provide a common understanding of what is being discussed. Let me illustrate what I mean. Most lists of competencies will include a category called "strategic thinking," a phrase that is meaningless without context. It can mean one thing to one person and something else to another. But if four or five leaders are engaged in a dialogue about a high-potential candidate and the question of that individual's capability for strategic thinking arises, all of the participants will arrive at a common understanding of the meaning. If, for example, the boss says the leader under discussion is an excellent strategic thinker because he devised a new compensation plan for the sales force, the other participants will quickly understand that although compensating the sales force can be a powerful motivational tool, it isn't really strategic thinking. They will adjust their opinion not only of the leader under discussion but also of the person who made the observation. If, on the other hand, someone notes that the leader devised a new method of segmenting customers that will allow the company to tailor its sales efforts, focusing the best sales teams on one set of customers while using the telephone or Internet to solicit other sets, the participants understand that the person really is demonstrating an ability to think strategically.

A dialogue session should involve at least four people who have direct knowledge of the leader, including the person's boss, several of the boss's peers, and preferably leaders at a higher level. HR should moderate the dialogue, bringing a high level of energy, probing for details and examples, guiding the discussion, and opening people's minds through questions and examples. At the start, the HR facilitator should explain the background of the exercise and state the ground rules. Initially each participant should make a list of positives about the person, and each person should have the chance to speak once before anyone speaks a second time.

The focus should be on getting the group to dig deeper and deeper to pinpoint the positives. There will be a natural tendency at first for the group to find flaws. That is a waste of time. It is the positives that make the person a valuable leader. If the positives aren't there, the negatives simply don't matter. You are not searching for what qualities the person *ought* to have but what the person already has and where he or she will flourish. The fact is, no one is perfect. Matching an individual's strengths—his natural abilities—with the nonnegotiable requirements of the job or the reshaping of a job is what produces great leaders.

If a flaw comes to light, it must be viewed in the context of the particular job and shouldn't necessarily take the leader off the list of high potentials. We all know leaders who were in jobs in which they appeared to be failing, only to excel when placed in a different kind of job. John Chambers didn't flourish and rise to CEO at the now-defunct Wang Laboratories, but when he went on to Cisco, a smaller company, he had a stellar career, taking the company from $149 million in revenue to $30 billion. Context matters.

Specificity is paramount. If someone says the leader has an executive presence, you have to push beyond vague impressions of what that means. Deconstruct it. The meaning may vary depending on which leader you're talking about. In one case, it may mean the leader can get people to listen to her and take her seriously. In another, it means the leader has perfected his PowerPoint presentation skills.

Once a list of twenty observations has been compiled, each participant should offer clear examples of how each behavior or trait manifested itself in actions, decisions, or behaviors. Going around the room, each is asked to confirm or disagree with what others have said. A list stated in everyday language can then be compiled of the person's natural talents on which there is widespread agreement. A second list can capture behaviors and traits that aren't so clear, and the group can watch for evidence of these. Finally, those talents and any traits or behaviors under continued debate should be reduced to a simple one-page summary that becomes the basis for development and assessment of the leader's fit for particular jobs.

The One-Page Summary

A good group discussion should yield a verbal portrait of an individual that captures the person's essence as a leader, emphasizing the talents and strengths and reflecting the unknowns while downplaying imperfections. The collective wisdom should be committed to paper, preferably before the session adjourns so nothing is lost. If the group has done its work well, it will have zeroed in on a handful of characteristics and capabilities that can be captured on one page.

One diversified company created a one-page profile following rigorous discussion of each of the leaders believed to have potential to be candidates for CEO succession seven to eight years out. Among them was Karen. She had a master's degree from Stanford Business School and had previously worked for two other companies. In her early jobs, she dealt with public demonstrations against her company, which was moving some of its operations overseas. She moved to the foreign country, then later took a job with another large company there. She ran the P&L for a subsidiary of the large company and, in that role, dealt frequently with the board of directors. Because the subsidiary was publicly held, she got the chance of a lifetime to deal with Wall Street at a young age.

She was recruited to run the smallest business unit of the large diversified company where she currently worked. The unit was losing money because a major player in the three-company industry kept cutting prices, squeezing margins industrywide. To make matters worse, that player had been founded by ex-employees of her business unit. The bitter rivalry was taking its toll, demoralizing employees. After two years in the job, Karen had rejuvenated the unit, and the company had decided to make her president of a division with three business units, a step toward becoming the CEO. She had not yet started the new job when a group of senior leaders, all familiar with her work, got together to share their observations and produced this one-page profile:

> Karen is highly disciplined. She is a turnaround specialist. She has a talent for dealing with external constituencies, including in a crisis. She is a clear communicator. She sets specific accountabilities and monitors them well. She is a good selector of functional people and is very capable of managing the intersections among silos. She is incisive, decisive, inclusive. She is hands on.
>
> Karen's bandwidth is limited because her focus is on one business in a turnaround. While she has had some success in finding growth opportunities, they have been very limited. She is a good selector of functional people; marketing vice president and operations manager were good hires. She is very capable of managing the intersections among silos. She did particularly well getting sales and operations to synchronize and meshing engineering and marketing. It is yet to be seen if she can select and manage business unit managers. She used her legal, finance, and HR staff to help her manage the single business. She has been hands on and relied on her domain knowledge. To be CEO of this diversified company, she will have to work through the business unit managers, coaching and developing them, calibrating their teams, and assessing each unit's unique issues, business model, competitive dynamics, and strategies. She must do this without smothering the business unit managers and without domain expertise.
>
> She will have to broaden her bandwidth from a single business to several simultaneously. Can she go beyond the existing businesses

and get ahead of the curve in jettisoning the ones whose market value she detects will continue to decline? Does she have the breadth and risk profile to think of new businesses in the market space allocated to her?

She takes psychological comfort in domain knowledge. She will have to build self-confidence without it by extracting the right information and asking the right questions to validate the business unit managers.

Karen is a Stanford grad. It is not clear she has that edge in her intellectual capacity. She can get immersed in lots of details and select the right ones to create a bigger picture. She is curious. When somebody is working with her and asking questions, she will reflect not only on the questions but also on the questioner's frame of reference to understand where the person is coming from.

It is not clear if she can develop people who are business unit leaders. The bets are that she is capable of it, but it remains to be seen. She needs to lead without being so hands on and with confidence outside her domain knowledge. She is being given the chance to do so in her new job. That is her next challenge. Her progress is being watched by several people.

The group had zeroed in on the capabilities and traits that stood out in Karen and also the areas that might require further development or testing.

The Growth Trajectory

Thomson keeps track of each leader's development with brief summaries of the leader's experiences and learning along with key tasks for them to work on and development goals. They find these brief, informal documents more useful than the notebooks full of data they used to gather. To track the big breaks in a leader's career, they plot each leader's sequence of jobs on a chart. Each job is a box. As the jobs increase in complexity, the boxes ascend from left to right, like stair steps showing progress over time. (See Figure 5.1 showing

Figure 5.1 How Thomson Tracks a Leader's Development

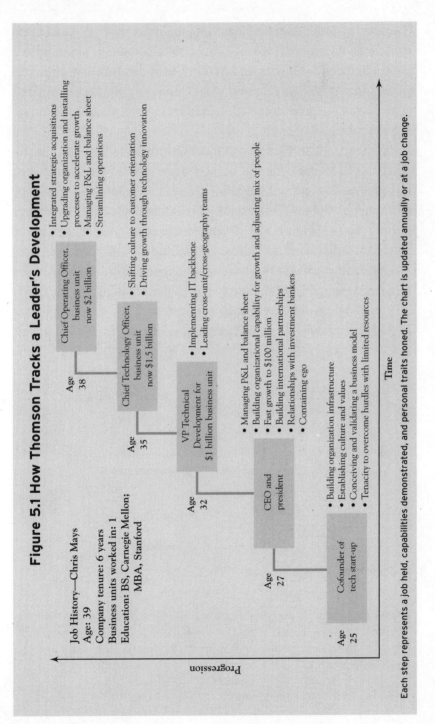

Job History—Chris Mays
Age: 39
Company tenure: 6 years
Business units worked in: 1
Education: BS, Carnegie Mellon; MBA, Stanford

Chief Operating Officer, business unit now $2 billion
- Integrated strategic acquisitions
- Upgrading organization and installing processes to accelerate growth
- Managing P&L and balance sheet
- Streamlining operations

Age 38

Chief Technology Officer, business unit now $1.5 billion
- Shifting culture to customer orientation
- Driving growth through technology innovation

Age 35

VP Technical Development for $1 billion business unit
- Implementing IT backbone
- Leading cross-unit/cross-geography teams

Age 32

CEO and president
- Managing P&L and balance sheet
- Building organizational capability for growth and adjusting mix of people
- Fast growth to $100 million
- Building international partnerships
- Relationships with investment bankers
- Containing ego

Age 27

Cofounder of tech start-up
- Building organization infrastructure
- Establishing culture and values
- Conceiving and validating a business model
- Tenacity to overcome hurdles with limited resources

Age 25

Progression

Time

Each step represents a job held, capabilities demonstrated, and personal traits honed. The chart is updated annually or at a job change.

Thomson's ladder chart.) The chart makes it easy to recall each leader's developmental history and sparks discussion about where he could go next. It has proved invaluable in determining what jobs a leader might be ready for and what other capabilities he needs to build. It gets updated after each recalibration or sooner if the leader changes jobs.

Companies can glean even more information if they plot the *trajectory* of a leader's growth. Some leaders grow faster than others; the angle of their growth trajectory may be very steep, as it was for Jeff Immelt, Michael Dell, and the other leaders mentioned earlier in this book (see Figure 5.2). A leader's trajectory can suggest when she is blocked, has hit her limits, or is taking off. It informs the next best move and adjusts the long-term expectation. If a leader has been overwhelmed and unable to rise to the challenge in the existing job, people will know within a year or two, but if the challenge was big enough and the leader is growing into it, she should stay in

Figure 5.2 What's the Leader's Growth Trajectory?

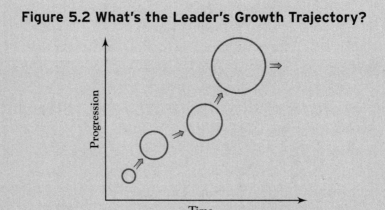

Track each leader's progress over time using the circle size to show expansion of capabilities. Consider the angle of the trajectory, why it is changing, and the pattern of growth. Trajectories are rarely linear. Some steps will be sideways or backward to allow for future expansion—for example, when a CFO is moved to a line job to manage a P&L and balance sheet.

the job longer—three to five years—and always long enough to see results.

Leaders fail to progress for myriad reasons, and some are not readily resolved. Personality traits, for instance, are nearly impossible to change, as are deeply ingrained behaviors. Emphasizing the positives in a leader doesn't mean disregarding a lack of performance or serious personal shortcoming. Bosses and HR departments must be willing to take people off the list of high-potential leaders even while they're identifying jobs where they can excel. Recruiting leaders from outside can compensate for the attrition and add fresh thinking.

There will be errors in assessing and refocusing leaders but far fewer when bosses and others pay attention to them and probe deep enough. As they do, the company's leadership and succession pool will deepen. Tracking the quality and quantity of that pool, as well as the progress of individual leaders, is part of the Apprenticeship Model. Colgate-Palmolive has processes and mechanisms to do both, which you will read about in the next chapter.

Chapter 6

MANAGING APPRENTICESHIP SYSTEMATICALLY

Every company has a formal routine for collecting financial data and sorting, sifting, and analyzing them. Most also gather and study information about product mixes and customers to help them pinpoint areas of strength and weakness. These systems give managers at all levels and the board of directors consistent and integrated data for making decisions based on hard facts. But few companies systematically compile comparably useful information about their leadership resources: the very foundation of business success.

Up to now, I've focused on how the Apprenticeship Model tailors leadership development to the individual. This chapter explains how the various elements of the model can be institutionalized and integrated, measured, monitored, and managed.

Can it really be done? Absolutely. Some companies do it every day. Colgate-Palmolive, for one, has mastered such a process and is enjoying tremendous success using it. Because its process is a working model that anybody can learn from, this chapter is devoted to it.

Colgate measures and manages its leadership talent as carefully as it does its market share, finances, brand equity, and physical inventory. It also frequently assesses its specific leadership needs to identify any gaps between the leaders it has in the pipeline and its emerging needs.

Companies setting out to adopt this approach should formalize mechanisms and methodologies that will enable them to do the following:

- Continually revisit the criteria and methods for identifying leadership talent to keep them attuned to external changes

- Assign individuals with leadership talent to a sequence of challenging and exciting work that builds future leadership capabilities while meeting current organizational needs

- Provide rigorous feedback to speed leaders' development

- Increase each leader's visibility within the company to solidify his or her connection with the company and allow other leaders to get to know the individual in depth

- Recognize and reward the best performers and adjust the talent tracks for those who don't meet the standards

- Periodically report on the numbers and types of leaders at various levels and assess any current or anticipated gaps

- Keep the board informed about the strength of the company's leadership bench, expose the board members to leaders several tiers below the CEO, and help them get to know succession candidates in depth

Let's look closely at how Colgate executes these tenets. Its methodologies and mechanisms are uniform across the globe, ensuring that the same process for identifying and developing leaders is used at every location where it does business and that it encompasses all functions—sales, marketing, information technology, human resources (HR), legal, supply chain, research and development, investor relations, communications, and finance—and not just line and general managers.

The criteria are explicit, so everybody has the same concept of what leadership potential looks like, but they are not set in stone. Colgate senior management has frequent discussions about them and constantly fine-tunes the mix in light of new requirements to meet competition, consumer tastes, shifting channels of distribution, and changing modes of communication to consumers in the more than 160 countries in which the corporation operates. As a result, the composition of its leadership pool is constantly changing to meet those needs. How does it know? Through reporting mechanisms that help senior management get a handle on the numbers and qualities of the leaders who are progressing. Recognizing that leadership is a key indicator of the company's health, management keeps the board engaged as well, just as it engages the board on financial matters. The CEO, Ian Cook, puts Daniel Marsili, global vice president for human resources, at the same level as all his direct reports in his working relationships.

In a company adopting this model, senior management will have to lead the effort. But the HR function should in no way feel disenfranchised. To the contrary, HR has a pivotal role in developing and maintaining the mechanisms and processes by which the organization tracks its leaders. The HR department is, as I have already stated, the trustee of the Apprenticeship Model. Its role isn't bureaucratic, filling out lots of forms. Rather, it is a value-adding role that requires working closely with business leaders to develop effective tools and processes and ensure that the model is applied with rigor and intellectual honesty. Ideally, HR professionals will become partners with business leaders, helping them to be mentors and offering informed judgments about individuals' leadership potential and suitability for jobs.

At a minimum, HR *must* ensure the following:

- That bosses give timely feedback to high-potential individuals that is specific, constructive, and actionable
- That bosses look beyond their narrow specialties to the broader pool of potential candidates when they select people
- That bosses promote people based on the concretely defined and nonnegotiable requirements of a job both today and tomorrow
- That bosses view leadership as a corporate resource. They must help leaders move from one place to another, testing and developing their skills, abilities, and leadership potential.

They cannot hoard talented people, shy away from taking risks on them, or ignore the development of people brought in under them

The first requirement is to make sure that all leaders understand that an important part of their jobs is to develop more leaders. They have to become adept at identifying leadership potential and then nurturing it through frequent feedback. But feedback alone isn't enough for developing high-potential leaders. HR must also ensure that leaders discuss each high-potential candidate through the dialogue process and arrive at a common understanding of his or her strengths and the obstacles to his or her progress. Once feedback and evaluation mechanisms are firmly established, the HR department can then begin the processes that lead to further development through movement into different jobs.

Colgate begins at the country level. At least once a year in smaller countries and often twice a year in larger ones, the leadership team devotes one or two days to a succession-planning discussion. What makes them effective is the careful preparation that precedes them. "If I'm the marketing director in a given country, long before we have the off-site discussions, I will have gone through all my development discussions with the people in my organization," explains Marsili. "I will have validated those discussions with what I had laid out in the previous year's planning sessions. I'll have updated the training and development plans for each person, looked again at their mobility situation, what their aspirations are, and what I think they are capable of doing. All that information goes into a database and generates a profile of a person that shows in a single page their personal information, work history and education, performance ratings, strengths and development needs, recommendations for their next two moves, what developmental actions we need to take, how they are meeting our requirements for managing with respect, and who their potential successors are."

Armed with all that information, a boss attends the off-site meeting prepared to discuss his or her people, get input from colleagues, and make some commitments. A typical result is that one person may be tapped to go to Colgate's New York headquarters. Another rising leader might be ready for some experience outside his subsidiary but for some reason may not be able to move at the moment. Because she is someone Colgate wants to retain and grow, the country team decides to send her to another subsidiary to observe a budget review. Not only does the experience provide her with new skills, she makes new contacts and sees how other people interact in a different cultural setting. Part of the discussion involves forecasting future vacancies within the country and developing lists of candidates to fill those vacancies when they occur. When the off-site session ends and people have committed to the agreed-on developmental actions, the HR department takes the responsibility for ensuring that they happen. This provides follow-through. Often the moves are internal to the country and can be done with a minimum of disruption and coordination with other countries or functions.

The same process occurs each year at the geographical division level—North America, Europe, Latin America, Asia, Africa, the Middle East, and at their specialty pet food division. The divisional leadership team begins by compiling the country subsidiary assessments. The subsequent discussion centers on reviews of top talent in both line management and functional areas. In the case of marketing, for example, the divisional leader reviews the top fifty or so marketing people in the country organizations and brings recommendations for their development to the annual discussion.

But there are some key differences in the methods and goals for the divisional discussions. Along with their internal planning-development moves, the leaders are also identifying global, regional, and local high potentials. The global high potentials become possible successors for key regional and global positions. Because those kinds of moves involve many stakeholders, the discussions are more complex. In finance, for example, the divisional finance leader will talk about best-available finance talent in various countries. But other functional and operational leaders will contribute as well.

The round-robin discussion is intended to develop multiple perspectives on a rising high potential's leadership abilities. The finance leader might, for example, extol the functional skills of her best person but learn that the manufacturing leader noticed in a meeting that he lacked the courage to speak up and represent the financial point of view. The meeting's outcome might include a commitment to give him feedback and more chances to interact with people in other functions.

The assessments and decisions flow to global functional management or global general management. Function high potentials are reviewed by the global function leaders, who create succession candidate pools while assessing the function's overall talent development challenges. High potentials destined for line jobs are reviewed by Colgate's senior team, consisting of the CEO, chief operating officer, division presidents, and global function heads. The senior team holds bimonthly review sessions, each dedicated to a single division or global function. The senior team's goal at these monthly reviews is fivefold:

- Understand the overall talent issues facing the organization
- Get acquainted with key people and high potentials and become familiar with potential leaders at lower levels
- Obtain an overall view of performance and potential
- Agree on development plans for key people
- Discuss candidates for key positions

In the case of a finance function review, the CFO before presenting to the senior team will have spent a day or two with the divisional financial heads from around the world. Each of those leaders will have evaluated their own regional or global high potentials and will have validated their assessments through cross-functional discussions within their own geographical areas. Armed with all that information, the CFO can have a detailed and relevant discussion with the senior team, including names and faces, development needs and plans, and the long-term potential of each person in the regional and global finance talent pool. He would explain who needed to be moved soon, who was in need of greater visibility, and who among them all might be considered as his own successor.

The final step in the process occurs at the board level where a personnel and organization committee—essentially an expanded compensation committee—gets presentations from the senior team about critical operational leaders who have a shot at the top jobs. The committee is just as interested in the development plans for those people as it is in their compensation. What's more, it looks beyond those on a path to the top to make sure that Colgate has a good balance of talent around the world by function and geography.

Board discussions about high potentials can take the form of surveys of the total talent pool, or they can be focused on specific candidates for specific jobs. A functional leader might be asked, for example, to name the three candidates most qualified to succeed him and the candidates who would, in turn, succeed them. Each direct report will be evaluated in terms of the development she would need to take the top functional job and ranked on the specific requirements for the job. The focus of these discussions is to determine the balance between strategic and tactical, between growth and profit, and between soft and tough and to identify who has a deep understanding of the business and the key drivers of it. Importantly, the board has an opportunity to meet with high-potential candidates for business presentations and to question and evaluate them.

One of the most important tenets of Colgate's talent identification and development process is that everyone everywhere is measured by the same standards, which Marsili refers to as a "success profile." The profile consists of three broad components: the ability to deliver results; demonstrated leadership competence, including the ability to continue to learn and improve and to help others learn and improve as well; and finally, the ability to "manage with respect and humanity" to distinguish the company and be a part of the community.

"We have consistent formats, and we use a consistent language to describe how people get things done and how they deliver results so that we have a level playing field everywhere," says Marsili. "If we have someone we consider a high potential in Vietnam, we want to be sure that person is of the same caliber as someone considered a high potential in Hungary or Brazil."

The details of each component change over time, usually in an evolutionary manner as the company adapts to changing circumstances in its markets and methods. But sometimes the change can happen rapidly. For example, "analytical skills and abilities" have always been part of the success profile. But Marsili says it recently became evident that many of Colgate's jobs were increasingly and rapidly becoming more analytical and that the company needed to stress the competency more. Also getting more emphasis now is change management. "A lot of people talk about change management, and it runs the risk of becoming overused," he says. "But people are dealing with so much ambiguity at work and in their daily lives that it is becoming a more significant competency."

Such shifts in emphasis alter the company's talent pool. Some potential leaders who were doing well before the new emphasis might not advance as well now. But the real impact is that once the company recognizes the new need, it can begin to spend time, energy, and dollars to develop the necessary competencies.

Putting global high potentials in the right jobs is a critical part of leadership development. Once pinpointed, these leaders embark on a rigorous series of challenging jobs aimed at filling in the gaps identified by Colgate's success profile. It isn't enough for them to move from one subsidiary to another in consistently bigger and more complex jobs. Instead, they are deliberately exposed to markedly different cultures and jobs. "If they come from a developed world environment, then we might want to give them a developing world experience," explains Marsili. "If they come exclusively from a marketing discipline, we might place them on a multifunctional team so that they can get more exposure to a sales environment. If they come from a highly structured supply-chain culture, we might want to get them into a developing world site where they're going to have to be very multifaceted, doing customer service, distribution—basically doing it all."

There is particular emphasis on the global movement of high potentials for commercial leadership jobs. The CEO, division presidents, the global head of sales, and Marsili meet monthly to decide who goes to what commercial job worldwide. And they look ahead to an individual's next two possible jobs and what needs to be done to prepare him or her for them. At the same time, they begin looking for that person's potential successors. They decide where to send the global high potentials based almost solely on what is best for their development and for the overall business. A decision made at that level trumps any efforts by lower-level bosses to hang on to their favored people, and the high-potential person knows that the decision is in his or her best interests.

"Too often, people think that the way to get ahead is to go from small to large," says Marsili, "but sometimes the kind of experience a person needs might be at a smaller unit on another continent. When you propose a move to a 'smaller sub,' the first question can be, 'Why is this right for my career?' So you have to have the right senior people give the person a candid set of explanations and discuss why the move is the best one to make. Then you have to deliver their future if they deliver for the company."

At each step, a global high-potential candidate gets the best constructive feedback and often an outside coach. Just as important, the high potentials are exposed as frequently as possible to Colgate's senior leadership. The company's senior managers travel frequently, and wherever in the world they go, they make time to meet with high potentials and their bosses to talk about how things are going for the developing leader. "It's a continuous process of learning and identifying and talking to and about people so senior managers really get to know them," Marsili says. "It's also a way to get them to identify with the company. It creates a strong connection to Colgate."

Rewards and recognition play an important role in the talent development process. "We're very mindful of ensuring that we are rewarding these top performers differently than we reward others," says Marsili. "We have metrics to ensure that these people are compensated at rates above the marketplace average, and we deploy special recognition tools, like providing them with stock ownership when they otherwise wouldn't be eligible."

Leaders at all levels participate periodically in what Colgate calls "visibility programs." In the first five years of their career, for example, young leaders might be invited to participate in a "Leadership Challenge" that brings high potentials from all over the world to New York for a week. The session starts with an Outward Bound session in the city, which helps them bond because they're coming from all over the world. Then during the course of the week, they meet every senior leader in the company and work on a real business issue confronting the company. They hear about the business challenges confronting Colgate, but they also absorb the lessons the senior people have learned over the course of their careers and the mistakes they've made. All the participants have a breakfast, lunch, or dinner with both the CEO and chairman to ask questions and get to know them.

High-potential leaders who have been with the company for ten or more years are invited to participate in Colgate's 20/20 Program, which is done in conjunction with an outside university. They stay together as a cohort for one year, also working on a significant Colgate business issue and, at the end, present their recommended business actions to the senior team. During the course of the program, which includes international trips and visits to universities, they meet often with senior leaders informally over breakfast or lunch.

Colgate makes a concerted effort to get high-potential leaders before the board of directors as early and often as possible. If, for instance, the vice president of marketing in the United States is leading a presentation to the board or one of its committees, she would include one or two high-potential marketing people. The very best contributors worldwide are selected by senior officers to receive Colgate's chairman's "You Can Make a Difference" Award for outstanding contributions to the company on a global basis. The winners are invited to attend the annual meeting and to have dinner with the board the night before the meeting.

Should the worst occur and a global high potential decide to leave the company, an emergency retention process kicks in. Every senior manager's long-term global growth program includes a goal of retaining 90 percent of the company's high potentials. If they fail to achieve that, they lose part of their compensation. When a high potential anywhere in the world submits a resignation, the CEO, chief operating officer, and global head of HR are alerted within twenty-four hours and launch efforts to discover why the high potential is leaving and what might be done to change his or her mind.

Monitoring the Leadership Pool

As you design various mechanisms and processes to implement the Apprenticeship Model, remember that you must go beyond identifying and developing individual leaders. You also have to monitor the depth and quality of the leadership pool overall, considering the following questions:

1. Is the pool of leaders diversified in age, gender, and functional abilities?

2. Is it focused on challenges and opportunities externally or focused almost exclusively on internal operations?

3. Does it include varied risk profiles: some leaders who seek only incremental change and some who are comfortable taking bigger chances?

4. Is it oriented toward innovation and finding opportunities, or is it largely defensive?

5. Does it consist almost entirely of heritage employees, or does it get infusions of newcomers?

6. Are the leaders in the pool focused on achieving individual excellence or leadership excellence?

You may have to adjust how you identify and develop individual leaders based on the answers to those questions. That information also should go to the board.

Boards need to compare periodic assessments of the depth and breadth of the company's current leadership pool against emerging leadership requirements, looking three to five years out. They should keep especially close tabs on the pipeline of future leaders in at least the top two levels of the organization and occasionally sample the leadership pool at lower levels, perhaps by visiting lower-level leaders onsite. Then they will know if the company is doing what it should to ensure a deep pool of leaders from which the board—and future boards—will ultimately have to choose a CEO. Making that choice is the subject of the next chapter.

Chapter 7

CHOOSING THE CEO WHO IS MOST LIKELY TO BE SUCCESSFUL

In June 2002, Mickey Drexler threw in the towel. As CEO of Gap, Inc., he had plied his merchandising expertise for nineteen years, making the retailer the icon of the booming market for casual dress and repeating his success with Banana Republic, Old Navy, Gap Kids, and Baby Gap. But competitors caught up and styles changed. By the turn of the century, Gap's growth slowed, then began to decline. Drexler tried to refocus the brand, but although many in the investment community were anticipating a Drexler-led turnaround, the family-dominated board was ready for a change. After two years of falling same-store sales, Drexler announced his retirement, and because the company had no internal successor, the board began an external search for a leader who could restore momentum.

Drexler had been at Ann Taylor before joining Gap, and his instincts for apparel retailing were legendary. But this time around the board thought Gap needed broad operating skills and marketing expertise, including the ability to segment consumers and knowing how to use information technology. They hired two top-notch executive recruiters and ended up with Paul Pressler, the Disney executive in charge of global theme parks and resorts. He was known to be cost-conscious, disciplined, methodical about research and analysis, and a team builder with an inclusive leadership style.

As Pressler sought to grab hold of the $13 billion company, merchandising decisions Drexler had made before his departure boosted sales and earnings for a while. Soon into his tenure, with the help of some former Disney executives he recruited, Pressler began to make changes of his own, notably to the culture and the supply chain. He mainly emphasized cost savings—for example, pushing to consolidate purchasing for Gap, Old Navy, and Banana Republic. But although that made financial sense, it blurred the distinctions between the brands and made them less responsive to their market segments. Pressler also moved to formalize processes, producing the unintended consequences of slowing decision making, adding complexity, and depending less on intuition—all in a business that demands quick decision making and constant trade-offs between design and merchandising informed by instincts about what consumers will buy.

After a brief honeymoon, corporatewide sales resumed their downward slide. A former Disney executive put in charge of the Gap brand didn't help. It became clear that Pressler, although admired for his strengths and past performance, was out of his element and did not have a handle on the clothing retail business. He left in January 2007. The board named one of its members, Robert Fisher (son of Gap's founder), interim chief executive and formed a search committee. This time when the committee spelled out the specific qualities they expected in a new leader, they included experience in apparel, saying they sought "a chief executive officer who has deep retailing and merchandising experience ideally in apparel, understands the creative process, and can effectively execute strategies in large, complex environments while maintaining strong financial discipline." That's not exactly what they got when in July 2007 the board selected Glenn Murphy for the top job. Murphy is an experienced retailer who has been CEO of a drugstore chain, CEO of a bookstore chain, and senior executive of a retail and wholesale food company, all in Canada. Directors of Gap apparently compromised on experience in apparel. Time will tell whether their decision is a wise one.

A board's judgment on the criteria for a CEO and the candidate who best meets them is a huge creator or destroyer of value. This is where the board really earns its keep: missteps can put the company so far behind it can never fully recover (think Kmart, which had four consecutive CEOs who failed, or Apple before Steve Jobs returned, which also had four consecutive CEOs who failed). Boards are acting sooner on a CEO who is stumbling, but asking a CEO to step down is easy compared with stopping the revolving door by selecting the right CEO in the first place. Although boards have begun to take this responsibility seriously, many lack a sufficiently rigorous methodology for improving their judgment on this ultra-important decision.

The Apprenticeship Model goes a long way toward deepening the pool of potential CEOs. But when a decision is imminent, the board must use tools and techniques designed to delve into the specifics of the CEO job and the suitability of succession candidates with great granularity and sharp focus. Heirs apparent and crown princes notwithstanding, the board must take hold of the selection process and approach it with a fresh and objective eye.

Three fundamental principles should guide the CEO succession process. The first is to recognize that the *CEO's job is quantitatively and qualitatively different from all other jobs*, including running a large business unit, a function, or a big geographical region. CEOs don't necessarily work harder or even smarter than they did in their former senior executive positions. Rather, they have to continually anticipate, in an uncommonly perceptive way and from a multitude of angles, what lies ahead and what must be done to seize opportunities or otherwise prepare for what they think is coming.

Business unit managers and country managers with profit-and-loss (P&L) responsibility will have many of the requisite CEO skills and traits. But they always have someone looking over and guiding, encouraging, and correcting them. The CEO, by contrast, lives in a world where no one provides guidance, encouragement, or correction. The military describes this aptly as "the loneliness of command." Harry Truman put it more bluntly: "The buck stops here." Regardless of the leaps the person has made in the past, no one is 100 percent prepared for the job. The only way to know for sure that a leader can rise to the challenge is to put him or her in the job. And because the job is the final test of a leader, the decision is never risk free.

Second, *no two CEO jobs are alike*. Every company has unique needs and opportunities that the CEO must recognize and act on. Even within the same company, the current CEO's job will be different from the previous one and the one that will follow. So *the concept of "fit" is paramount*. The board has to determine what qualities the company most needs in its leader at that time and then to find the match. This principle puts an end to the "best athlete syndrome," where boards vie for leaders who have performed spectacularly well elsewhere on the assumption that they can be winners at their company, too. It is a fallacy to think that a CEO can succeed in any business. Leaders who make their careers largely on cost cutting, for example, tend to develop a psychology and brain architecture that makes it hard for them to deal with the uncertainty inherent in pursuing top-line organic growth. Further, they tend to surround themselves with other cost cutters.

The third principle is that *CEOs are people, complete with their share of human flaws*. The search for a perfect leader is like chasing the rainbow. The key is to understand the candidates in their entirety, to pinpoint the talents that make a particular leader stand out as the best possible person to lead the business at that time. The board must come to terms with candidates' imperfection, detect any fatal flaws, and make a judgment call about which leader seems strongest in the areas that count most. It would be great to have a top-notch operating person with a keen strategic mind, but it may be completely unrealistic. Do you go with the person who is strategic but less disciplined in operations or the other way around? Making this judgment is an awesome responsibility because the fate of the company and many people's lives depend on it. Boards have to draw out the best thinking of all of their members and make this judgment *collectively*.

The board must approach the CEO succession decision with passion and intensity, devoting a lot of time and energy to it years in advance. The seniormost human resources (HR) executive and, in most cases, the incumbent CEO should be involved, not only to design the tools but also to contribute to the discussion of the business and the candidates and to manage the tricky issues that arise as the list of potential CEO contenders gets whittled down.

Although many boards take succession seriously, I have observed that much of what they do lacks the rigor they are striving for. Discussions about candidates tend to quickly focus on personality traits and, after that, the person's experience, with achievements merely sprinkled in, usually anecdotally. Directors begin to support a person without digging deeper. This behavior is often triggered by a CEO who is emotionally invested in one candidate and tries to sell the board on the person informally and behind the scenes. Even as the board welcomes the CEO's input, directors must take responsibility for amassing all the facts about the candidates and business issues and not make partially informed judgments.

Sometimes directors pick up an impression in their interaction with a candidate that overshadows everything else about the leader. It could be a positive or a negative—for instance, a splashy and successful marketing campaign, a mishap on a security analyst's call, or procrastination in making a decision about a direct report. That one piece of information taints their view of the person and prevents them from giving the leader a thorough vetting. In other cases, directors interpret the search criteria differently, and because they don't articulate them, those differences are unresolved. Then a few key directors drive the search based on the interpretations they have in the back of their minds.

The Rewards of a Painstaking Process

In advance of a planned decision, the governance (or another) committee, preferably with the help of HR, should develop the process by which the succession decision will ordinarily be determined. Process isn't everything, but a well-designed one helps ensure rigor and objectivity and eliminates some of the human problems that come into play when, say, a CEO or dominant director pushes for his favorite candidate. Boards should take great care in designing and following it.

Few have taken more care than the board of Blue Cross Blue Shield of Michigan (BCBSM) did in choosing its latest CEO in 2004–2005. Although the board's size and makeup made the assignment especially challenging, the remarkable details of their process, which I observed firsthand, hold lessons for any board.

BCBSM started in 2004, a year before the CEO was due to retire. The thirty-five-member board, under the leadership of Greg Sudderth, had representation from many distinct constituencies, including the public (governor appointees), labor unions, large company management like the automakers, smaller company management, health care providers, and the seniors of the state. The board could not afford to let the decision become a tug-of-war among factions because the next CEO would need broad support to be able to accomplish anything meaningful. To ensure that the board ended up on common ground, BCBSM created an eight-phase process that would ensure rigor and objectivity. "Start together, end together" became the mantra, and disciplined adherence to the process was the means for acting on it.

The board began the organizing phase in mid-2004 by outlining a search process, setting a timeline, and agreeing on who would do what. The executive committee, a group of twelve board members representing all the constituencies, would serve as the search committee, and the board in its entirety would be the selection committee. The search committee would look inside the company first, with the help of HR head George Francis, his key staffer Cathy Sinning, and other staff members. The board also decided to use a third-party facilitator, whom they carefully picked for his experience and seasoned judgment on business, people, and corporate governance issues.

The committee moved quickly through the organizing phase to begin the search in September 2004, with its first update to the full board scheduled for mid-October and the final decision targeted for four months out. The short time frame was a scheduling challenge, especially because the group insisted that every search committee member take part in every single discussion so that all would get the same information at the same time. Meetings were scheduled on weekends, early mornings, or late evenings—whatever it took to keep the process moving swiftly. Elaborate meeting notes were kept for those one or two instances when somebody absolutely could not be there.

Phase two, information gathering, began with two key questions: What would it take to succeed as CEO in the dynamic, politically charged health care environment, and how did the search committee feel about the company's current direction?

The committee interviewed dozens of experts, including political leaders, the president of the Blue Cross Blue Shield Association, senior executives, and the chair of the statewide bargaining committee for the United Auto Workers union local that represented BCBSM employees. In advance of each interview session, they sent participants a set of questions designed to stimulate discussions. That set the stage for reaching a shared understanding of the organization and the environmental context. The facilitator played a key role in getting everyone on the same page by pointing out contradictions that were still unresolved, asking questions that pushed for a more nuanced view of the externals, and challenging assertions that lacked supporting evidence. That common view began to suggest the skills, traits, and attributes the CEO would need. Finishing up in January 2005, they moved on to phase three: nailing down first the criteria for the CEO, and then assessing the internal candidates.

Defining the criteria for a CEO is always tougher than it first appears. Boards have to push beyond the generic characteristics every chief executive should possess (the givens) to understand the specific challenges of that position at that time. These are the nonnegotiable criteria. The nonnegotiables will also suggest some personal traits associated with them—for instance, a company facing major internal change and repositioning in the market needs someone able to think broadly and creatively and willing to take risks. It almost always takes several iterations to arrive at a set of criteria broad enough to ensure that nothing important is being overlooked but also specific enough to point to exactly the right person. It's easy to get lost in the myriad givens and never get to the guts of what the person has to be able to do.

The givens BCBSM specified, which anyone in the pool had to meet, were

- Passion, honesty, authenticity, integrity, and principle-centered leadership
- Good communication skills
- Confident without being arrogant
- Emotionally stable

Then the committee moved on to other criteria. Each search committee member suggested some, then they divided them into personal traits and skills and the nonnegotiables. The personal traits were

- Inclusiveness
- Promoter of diversity in the workplace
- A political consensus builder, able to balance the needs of various constituencies
- Advocate of a viewpoint important to BCBSM
- Role model, coaches and develops people
- Able to become a thought leader statewide and nationally
- Customer oriented

Deciding on the nonnegotiable criteria took the most time. From committee members' suggestions, the group created a list of roughly ten nonnegotiable criteria, some of them implying different priorities for the business. They did not want to combine them for fear that they would merely create poor compromises or make them overly generalized. Instead, guided by the chairperson and the outside adviser, they broke into small groups to discuss and sharpen them, then reconvened, then separated again. After three rounds, the committee had developed strong, distinct options that they could then debate and choose from. In the end, the committee narrowed the list to four imperatives for a new CEO representing the committee's common view of the general direction the company needed to go:

- Take the initiative and work with appropriate external constituencies to actively help shape the highly uncertain and politicized external landscape. Define a clear, focused strategy in this complex and evolving health care environment.
- Determine the business model for BCBSM going forward, being fully fiscally prudent in the context of autos (a major customer), dwindling membership, rising cost of health care, and increasingly intense competition.
- Be good at execution, selecting the best people, fostering diversity, building the best leadership team, and creating a corporate culture of change and innovation with product and process simplification.
- Develop a national focus, grow the business, and maintain quality and safety in a vibrant health care delivery system.

In phase four, the search committee, working with the incumbent CEO, Richard Whitmer, identified four internal candidates. All were senior vice presidents or higher and familiar because they dealt frequently with the board. Some directors had their favorites and might even have made encouraging comments to them. But the process was designed to get the search committee beyond preconceived ideas and emotional commitments by walking through the candidate assessments together. It also put the newer board members on an equal footing with those who had long tenure and knew the candidates well. The process would create a common knowledge base for weighing each candidate against the nonnegotiable criteria. Discussions were open, and the committee chair made sure that every candidate got a fair hearing. Over the course of several meetings, the committee analyzed the candidates' previous actions, decisions, and behaviors; pooled their judgments about what particular talents each leader had demonstrated; and explored how each would fit with what was needed to succeed in the job.

Most boards would want to involve all their members in such discussions, but BCBSM's directors agreed this wasn't practical, given the board's size. Instead, the twelve-member search committee made frequent detailed reports to the full board, so all thirty-five members were operating with the same common understanding at all times.

A lot of care went into the subsequent in-depth interviews with the candidates, and here, too, the committee took extra pains to ensure objectivity by keeping all members equally involved and informed. The goal was to go far beyond the usual content of such interviews: formulaic questions about experience, education, training, and the like. The group engaged the candidates in meaty discussions to fully understand who each person really was and what each could bring to the table, including how they approached problems, how flexible they were, how they went about making decisions, and how they thought about strategy.

The interviews, conducted offsite over one weekend at an airport hotel, were identical in format and length: ninety minutes. The twelve directors sat in one room at a U-shaped table and divided themselves into groups of three. As each candidate came in and sat in the middle of the U, one group of directors took the lead in asking structured questions the committee had agreed on. About forty-five minutes was allotted for those. The other members listened, then had the chance to ask additional questions, occasionally caucusing in their small groups to share their observations and feelings on the spot. Those quiet conversations between questions helped directors crystallize their thinking and further questions, and as they did, previous opinions and politics subsided. Candidates did not get any questions in advance because the committee wanted to see how the leaders reacted under pressure, but the committee was respectful of the candidates at all times. In scheduling the interviews at a hotel airport, for instance, they made sure the candidates, who all knew each other, would not cross paths.

Going in, directors preferred an inside candidate because they believed the company was on the right trajectory, but they were prepared to expand their search to outside candidates in a fifth phase if necessary. As it turned out, the committee agreed that any of the four individuals could be a good CEO. So phase four would culminate with the committee's CEO recommendation to the full board.

Well versed by now in the demands of the job and its external context, the committee shifted its debate from discussion about what each candidate had to offer to which candidate best fit those criteria. As a rule, when the nonnegotiable criteria are clear and specific, they point to one individual. This held true at BCBSM. Following another round of rigorous discussion, a consensus emerged. The attributes the committee had pinpointed in this person included the following:

- A "people person" who was yet not bound by the existing culture.
- A great relationship builder, committed to engaging external and internal stakeholders. He knows the local and state political scene and is the best person there is when it comes to political constituencies. He is also skilled in building appropriate consensus to shape the BCBSM future.
- He is not part of the problem; he is always part of a potential solution.
- He commands respect.
- He has not demonstrated conclusively that he can transform such a large organization, but he selects and retains great people.

Finally, it was time to bring the recommendation to the board, discuss it in depth, and reach a decision. This was phase six. At a meeting in mid-March, the third-party adviser walked the board through the search committee's process to date and presented the in-depth candidate profiles. The information was not entirely new to the board because they had been kept fully informed at every juncture.

Prepared in advance were four press releases, one announcing each candidate as CEO, to fend off rumors and to prepare for any outcome the board might reach. The search committee then made its recommendation: Dan Loepp. Some board members were visibly surprised, no doubt because the candidate commonly perceived as the front runner was passed over. But as discussion ensued, the logic behind the decision became more and more compelling. When this diverse thirty-five-member board took a vote, their choice was unanimous.

The thorough and thoughtful process had given the board's work substance and rigor. Directors took the time to learn about the critical issues of the business, the industry, the various constituencies, and the regulators in Washington, D.C., so they had a deep understanding of what the next CEO would face. The profiles of the candidates were detailed and balanced and, most important, based on factual evidence, leaving little room for a board member to lean toward or lobby for a favorite candidate. The information led each and every director to see that, indeed, there was one best fit—albeit not a perfect fit (there never is). The board called the selected candidate into the boardroom, where he was met with a standing ovation. It was, as Francis puts it, "a heady moment."

The candidates who were not chosen were treated with the utmost respect. The process and timing had been outlined for them early on, so they never had to wonder what would happen next or what they were expected to do when. Each was informed of the decision right away. Naturally they were disappointed, but the objectivity of the process made it a little easier for them to accept the new CEO as their boss. After that, it was just a matter of dotting the *i*'s and crossing the *t*'s in phases seven and eight: drafting and getting approval of the CEO agreement, making the employment offer, and discussing transition issues.

Notable as they are, the mechanics of the BCBSM CEO selection process are less important than the guiding principles: create a process that includes deep exploration of the company's issues and gets everyone on the search committee (and the board) on the same page with a precise understanding of the external context; translate that general discussion into specific, differentiated *nonnegotiable* criteria that will make or break the company; identify candidates inside and outside the business; assess them thoroughly through dialogue among the board members, conducted by an outside facilitator, if necessary, to arrive at a complete picture of each individual. *Then find the best fit*. Above all, keep talking until the nuances and specifics are in sharp focus and individual judgments converge. Never forget: process alone is not enough. Content matters.

Every company also must be prepared to make an equally sound succession decision on a moment's notice to prepare for what some refer to as "the beer truck scenario": Who would lead the company if the current CEO were suddenly struck by a beer truck? Some boards keep the name of the person the CEO recommends as successor in an envelope just in case, bearing in mind that the name must be a closely guarded secret, perhaps locked away. That name should be reviewed at least once a year. Some boards opt to have a director become interim CEO while the board conducts a formal search, an approach that fills the leadership void while allowing for a thorough vetting of succession candidates. The governance committee should map out a game plan before such an emergency arises.

Determining the Criteria

It should be clear from the stories of Gap and BCBSM that nothing is more important than pinning down the right criteria for a new CEO. A company adopting the Apprenticeship Model will revisit its leadership criteria regularly—for example, during talent reviews presented to the board. But directors setting out to choose a successor must sharpen their thinking about the company's fundamental needs. Many boards go wrong by relying too much on the givens, which are the usual content of generic job descriptions and search criteria. Because every company's situation is different from that of other companies, and more and more often different from year to year, the right criteria will be unique for each new succession.

Any CEO today will face a daunting array of variables, uncertainties, and risks. She must constantly make decisions, some of major consequence, without ever having all the information she would like. The CEO is basically placing an informed and intuitive bet when she decides to make a major acquisition or to change the company's focus and strategy. She has the responsibility of deciding how to deal with any number of external constituencies, some of them at times hostile and with conflicting agendas, including shareholders, legislators and regulators, and various special interest groups. And she no longer works for just one boss but for a group of part-time board members. To succeed in such an environment requires a complex and intense interplay of psychological and personality traits that test the person's capacity to deal with uncertainty and ambiguity. Sooner or later a CEO will be tested by circumstances or surprises she has never experienced before. Resilience in the face of adversity and a willingness to change to meet new conditions are hallmarks of any successful CEO and qualities the board must seek.

I have been studying CEOs for much of my life, and one thing I've observed is that the best of them have in common an intellectual edge that distinguishes them from the run-of-the-mill CEO. That edge is visible in various traits, two of which stand out. First, they can delve into a mass of numbers, data, and other evidence, pinpoint precisely and clearly the core of an issue or problem, and abstract qualitative insights. Second, they are able to judge the people working with and for them precisely, identifying their specific talents and the context in which those talents work better. Boards should look for these specific intellectual capabilities.

Boards also have to dig deeper into their company's situation, pushing and probing, asking their most incisive questions, bringing in outside experts if necessary, until they have a clear picture of what a new CEO must do well. They need to iron out any underlying disagreements about company direction or gaps in understanding the business and its external context. Given the intense demands on any CEO, this probing will likely elicit numerous challenges, but the board must decide which desirable traits and skills are most likely to be critical three years, five years, and even ten years out. The work cannot stop until the board has boiled it all down to the three or four specific skills and abilities that are critical to the company's future. These are the nonnegotiables.

In 2001, when Bank of America faced a succession decision, the board concluded that the company would need someone very different from the current CEO, Hugh McColl. It wasn't that McColl hadn't performed superbly. A skilled deal maker, he had made dozens of acquisitions that transformed the little-known Charlotte-based North Carolina National Bank first into a regional powerhouse, NationsBank, then into the largest U.S. consumer bank when it merged with California-based BankAmerica to create Bank of America.

The right successor, the board thought, would be someone who could bring all those mergers and acquisitions together into a coherent whole. Deal making was no longer the priority; operating experience and ability to put the business on a trajectory of long-term value creation was. Those criteria pointed to Ken Lewis, a company veteran and president of the bank's Consumer and Commercial Banking division. After being named CEO, he suspended the acquisition spree and concentrated on organic growth, focusing on market segmentation and the cross-selling needed to achieve it. His efforts, supported by the board, were successful. After a hiatus of roughly two years, the bank was again ready to take on major acquisitions, and it merged with FleetBoston.

The point is that when the set of criteria for a new CEO looks like that of any other company, the board has not done its job. When the criteria are specific and unique to the business needs at the time, they will provide useful clues about which of the candidates is most likely to succeed.

It's dangerously easy to lose sight of the nonnegotiable criteria when the full range of hoped-for qualities is listed. One way to deal with that is to categorize the criteria for a new CEO, as BCBSM did. Creating a category of givens can help get a lot of items out of the way that are important but not useful in distinguishing the right leader because every candidate should possess them. The nonnegotiables are all-important. The WellPoint board not only articulated what those pivotal capabilities were but also explained in a four-page document exactly what each capability was and why it was important to the business. In addition to givens and nonnegotiables, the document also included a third category for more targeted personal traits and skills. It was understood that candidates were unlikely to meet all the criteria, but discussing them and committing them to paper ensured that the board had a shared ideal to hold candidates up against. The nonnegotiables were the centerpiece, and the givens were basically grounds for disqualification.

Identifying Candidates in Time

Even if you have not adopted the Apprenticeship Model, you should start succession planning in earnest at least five years ahead of the CEO's planned departure. The focus then will be on insiders first, usually on candidates who report directly to the CEO. The number of leaders identified in this pool will vary from company to company and with proximity to the departure, but usually between two and five candidates will emerge in the several years leading up to a planned succession. This is when some boards will notice that all of the candidates are of a similar mind-set and age, probably in their early fifties. They might want to supplement the list by picking people who are younger, even if they are two levels below the CEO. If the Apprenticeship Model or something similar has been in place for some time, the potential CEO pool is likely to be younger, more diverse, and more closely matched to the company's evolving needs.

Relationships among the candidates, who are colleagues as well as competitors for the CEO job, can be tricky and pose challenges in retaining these talented leaders. The board has to keep its feelers out to ensure that the CEO is minimizing any unhealthy tensions and watch for changes in behavior as the candidates feel the pressure to compete. A candidate who undermines a colleague, hoards resources, or engages in grandstanding reveals underlying character traits that probably should take her out of the running. That's why it's wise not to narrow the field too far in advance of the CEO's retirement.

Signaling one candidate as the clear front-runner too long before the CEO is ready to leave causes problems, too. He may become impatient in the number two position and lobby against the CEO before he's fully prepared to take the helm. The current CEO candidate is also likely to be courted by headhunters. Or the CEO might be subconsciously holding on to the baton, saying "Joe isn't ready yet" when in fact he is. Boards have to be attuned to such issues and prepared to address them. They also must intensify their involvement in these leaders' careers to ensure that the assignments they get can fill gaps and answer questions the board has about them. They should know the specific plans for all leaders in the running, monitor their progress, and probe to find out what may be blocking them.

In some cases, the board has to take decisive action. In early 2007, a large, well-known company had a CEO succession candidate who had been instrumental in shaping his company's strategy, and the board saw him as the top contender for the CEO job two years out. Meanwhile, however, he had numerous attractive offers coming his way: three offers to be CEO of other companies and one to partner with the CEO of a private equity company. The board had a conundrum. Should it continue with the incumbent CEO for two more years and let the candidate move elsewhere, or should it have the CEO pass the baton now? The incumbent had led the company to peak performance and was continuing to do the CEO job admirably, but the board thought that the succession candidate was somewhat better suited to take the company forward. It was a tough decision, but in this case the board persuaded the current CEO to retire.

In many companies it's assumed that the chief operating officer (COO), if the company has one, and the chief financial officer

(CFO) will be candidates for the CEO's job. A COO may be in the running, but it should not be automatic. Good COOs are masters of detail who can do great work on the operational side. But they often lack the cognitive abilities and risk profile required to be CEO and rarely face the same pressure to deal with the external issues, investors, or even the board. The longer a COO has been in his job, the harder it will be for him to broaden his perspective enough to assume all of the complexities and uncertainties a CEO faces. It's different, of course, if the COO has been in the job as part of the preparation to become CEO.

The board might suggest that a COO with CEO potential be asked to run an autonomous division, where his responsibilities would include repositioning and growing the business. There are some practical problems in recommending such moves, though, one of which is the COO's perception that it is a step backward. Before any attempt to force a move, the board should think long and hard about the COO's likelihood of raising his cognitive skills and bandwidth for strategy.

A CFO may very well have the ambition and even potential. Certainly, if the company is undergoing restructuring, changing its portfolio mix, has deep financial problems, or has adopted a growth strategy that depends on mergers and acquisitions, a CFO may be a strong candidate, especially if he has demonstrated people skills and other aptitudes necessary for the top leadership post. But to fully prepare the person to be CEO, the CFO should have a line job that will provide an opportunity for him to exercise broader skills. Granted, the CFO might see such a move as a loss of prestige, so he'll have to understand the benefits. The board has to know what it expects in the way of development, follow his progress closely, and allow enough time for him to grow into the new job and either show results or not.

As time passes, the internal pipeline may shrink because some candidates fail to develop further or because changes in the company's situation shift the requirements for the next CEO. The board should then urge the CEO to bring in and test outsiders or to expand the search to insiders who are one or two rungs down. It may be necessary to create jobs for these contenders, although the board and CEO should think through the consequences. One company thought it would be a good idea to test a promising leader by creating a job between her current post and the CEO job. The result was an additional layer through which information and decisions got filtered. This went on for two years, and some key people began to leave, causing execution to suffer. The CEO rectified the problem just in time.

Neither the board nor the CEO can make promises to people as they move them into jobs they have not chosen or may not want, but they have to explain the importance of the moves and the consequences of not taking the assignment. One company faced a sticky situation in trying to develop a person the board and the CEO believed had CEO potential but no line experience. Jake had joined the company with a consulting background and worked closely with the strategic planner for years, where his creative, agile mind had caught the attention of the senior team. In the board's routine discussions of CEO succession, which was still more than five years away, Jake came up on the radar screen. What, they wondered, should we do to develop him?

The company had only two businesses, the largest and strategically most important of which was on shaky ground. The person running it had a great reputation with the press and was still relatively new in the job, so no one wanted to displace him, yet results were not coming through. The CEO and head of HR had the idea to put Jake in charge of a large segment of the business. That sounded good to Jake, provided he could report to the CEO. But the CEO knew that the head of the business wouldn't accept the arrangement, and he didn't want to force the issue for fear of losing him. So Jake had to report to the business head with nothing more than assurances from the CEO and the board that they would track him. He had to demonstrate several things: that he could help diagnose the problems, figure out the solutions, and take hold of the organization's social system, which he had not had to do in his previous staff job. Jake accepted the move and adjusted his psychology to attack the job with full force. The story is still being written, but so far he is still considered to have CEO potential, and the board has been asking about him and interacting with him at frequent intervals.

Making the Match

A board gets a rich base of knowledge for evaluating potential CEOs by spending time with them not only in formal settings like the boardroom but informal ones, like the golf course. There are plenty of ways to create those opportunities. Some boards, for instance, schedule dinners with younger executives the night before the board meeting and arrange table seatings conducive to relaxed conversation. But when the actual succession decision is months, not years, away, boards should in essence start from scratch to ensure that they are doing the most objective, up-to-date assessment of the two critical parts of the decision: what the job demands and who is best suited to do it.

As the board conducts those deep discussions about what the company is facing and how that translates into nonnegotiable criteria, the directors, CEO, and the head of HR will identify the small set of leaders who are in the ballpark. This is generally not a time for surprises, but unexpected things happen when smart people reflect together. It takes just one director to say "Janet might not have the strongest track record in operations, but she took hold of that troubled Asian division so quickly" for the board to give a leader, even a level below, a closer look.

This is also the time to reconsider the insider-versus-outsider issue. Most companies would prefer to select an inside candidate, for several reasons. First, the information about outsiders is often incomplete. Second, despite the higher risk of hiring a leader they know less about, boards often have to pay them more for signing bonuses and to make them whole on equity stakes they give up at their former employers. Third, CEOs hired from outside often change teams, direction, and culture, and if those changes are misguided, the next leader has to change them yet again, this time in the face of an organization that is cynical, confused, or just plain tired. Such tumult often causes defections of talent at the top and triggers a downward spiral with worsening prospects for finding and attracting a chief executive with the skills to set things right.

On the other hand, there are times when an outsider has a clear edge, when, for instance, the company needs

- A turnaround (think Alan Mullaly at Ford)
- To restore credibility (Ed Breen at Tyco)
- To undertake a culture shift (Randy Tobias at Eli Lilly)
- A radical change in strategic direction (Fred Kindle at ABB)

The board must probe deeply into what the candidate has actually accomplished to better discern her capabilities and personality. It's fair to ask an external candidate what he has in mind for the company, and the board should try to read between the lines of the answer. If the person plans to recruit a team of people, perhaps some he's worked with before, or has brought a team along with him in the past, his modus operandi could be to apply the same "fix" to every leadership job he's in. It might not be the fix you need. That may have been the case with Pressler at Gap.

For all their previous exposure, directors' knowledge of individual candidates is likely to be uneven. Pooling their insights is absolutely essential. The best understanding of people emerges from open discussion in group settings, focused on drawing out every observation and unspoken instinct about each succession candidate and arriving at a collective view. Perfunctory reference checking and interviews by a few search committee members for several hours at a time don't provide boards the depth of insight needed to make this most important decision. Specificity is key. It's not good enough to say she is operational, he's strategic, she's a deal maker, or he's great at execution. The board has to get below the level of generalities by drawing on what the leaders have actually done and how they actually behave. At BCBSM, the search committee had known their candidates for years. They nevertheless spent many hours preparing exactly the right questions to ask in the interviews and then spent days exchanging their views and probing each other to try to nail down exactly what each individual had to offer.

The leadership of such discussions is crucial, especially when a process is new to the board. The leader has to be sensitive to who is or is not speaking and draw out those who are reluctant. She can do this by asking questions or asking for an alternate view. She can tone down a dominant person by restating what was said or asking for specific examples of actions and decisions to illustrate whatever point the person is making. For example, she could follow an assertion that candidate A is a brilliant strategist with the simple suggestion, "Let's see the range of strategic skills through some examples."

Boards should involve all their members in assessing the CEO candidates. Sometimes it's useful to increase the informality by breaking the board into smaller groups of two or three directors to share their views of the candidates. Then when the full board reconvenes, the groups can compare their findings. Following the lengthy discussions, the board should create a written profile of each candidate. If the interviews and discussions have been sufficiently deep and specific, each profile will cover wide-ranging variables— from the person's views about the business to how she handles stress—and provide an unmistakably clear depiction of who the candidate is as both a leader and a human being. It should be plain to see what each candidate uniquely has to offer.

The board of a health care company determined that their next CEO would have to be able to grow earnings per share by double digits each year, recruit and develop leaders, make information technology a competitive advantage, and focus on both innovation and productivity, even if it required a major organizational transformation. And, of course, they wanted the quality that is more or less a given for any health care company today, the ability to work with multiple external constituencies. Their wish list might sound nearly impossible to meet, but it reflected the realities of what it would take for the business to thrive.

When the board compared the extensive profiles of the internal candidates against the carefully constructed nonnegotiables, one person stood out. Directors had observed among other things that he had a broad aperture for viewing the business and its external context and loved external relations. He had demonstrated an unusual capability to manage noncustomer external groups. This person knew how to deliver results and had good instincts for making money. He was a good selector of people and was good at cutting his losses on people. One of his outstanding qualities was being able to think through second-, third-, and fourth-order consequences of decisions. He was a consensus seeker but didn't hesitate to make tough calls on people. He was a creative thinker and a continuous, fast learner. While the items in the profile didn't specifically mention technology, the insights into the candidate's personality and mental capacity suggested that he would have no trouble understanding how to apply it.

The profile of another contender who didn't make the final cut also brought out many strengths, such as the drive and ability to deliver results, capacity for working well with and developing people, domain expertise of the industry, and openness to new ideas. But there were subtle yet significant differences between her and the board's ultimate choice. Her record had demonstrated that she made incremental moves and missed some emerging trends where big bets were required. The board got the sense that she was less comfortable with the shifting complexity and had difficulty getting to the core issues. It was clear to them that when tough circumstances arose, she would likely make defensive rather than offensive moves. Accomplishments on a resume and two-hour interviews simply don't allow the board to get to that kind of nuanced characterization of a leader in which so much will be vested.

Evaluating outsiders is even trickier because so much less is known about them. It's all the more important to dig for insights with comprehensive interviews and personal reference checking, including asking specific questions, followed by group discussions. Boards should be especially skeptical of a great reputation stoked by public relations. They must exercise due diligence in getting to the specifics of what a superstar has to offer regardless of how highly he is esteemed by others. And don't forget that even a leader who has been tremendously successful at two or three other companies may be all wrong for yours. A minor flaw can become fatal in a different context.

It's unlikely any one candidate will meet all the nonnegotiable criteria. That's when the board has to make the hard choice about which way to tilt—which are the *most* nonnegotiable, and therefore which candidate do we choose? Do you choose the leader who is great at execution but shows no strategic agility or the brilliant strategist who is loose in managing operations? Do you choose the strong operating person or the leader who can deal with Wall Street? Do you take a chance on a terrific leader who lacks global experience? Or on one who can do it all but is insensitive to public opinion? How important is domain knowledge? This is the ultimate test of the board's wisdom and judgment. I have seen boards face these recurring dilemmas in making this judgment call, and there are no clear-cut solutions.

Helping the New CEO Succeed

Becoming a CEO is a big leap for leaders, even those who have followed a thoughtfully designed career path. The CEO must take hold of the job within the first three to six months, and the board should provide whatever help they can, whether it's coaching from a seasoned director or concrete suggestions for how to complement the CEO's expertise. The board should also realize that it can be a challenge for the new CEO to build a working relationship with them. Chances are she knows the board well when she assumes the post, but familiarity is not the same thing.

Boards should be sure their new CEO is seeking and listening to their input but not completely deferring to them either. A CEO may feel so grateful to the board and perhaps to one or two dominant directors for choosing her that she lets them overstep their governance role. Consider, too, the impact of letting the outgoing

CEO retain a board seat. For legal or government issues or for the sake of customer relationships, there are some exceptions that make sense, but even then the arrangement should be limited to two years at the most. The board may be more comfortable with the former CEO, but the important issue is how soon the new CEO can be comfortable with the board and vice versa. Most often the outgoing CEO's presence slows the transition and undermines the new CEO's authority, especially when it comes to making bold moves that might have to include undoing the predecessor's decisions: cutting favorite projects, say, or divesting an acquisition. These are painful discussions for the former CEO.

One goal of the candidate assessment process is to unearth whatever questions the board has about each candidate and to identify any gaps and potential blind sides. Those areas warrant particular scrutiny. Is the successor able to overcome his strong operating orientation to forge a new strategy? Is he taking steps to create the culture change required? Is her learning motor gearing up or down? Here executive sessions can be useful for directors to provide thoughtful feedback rather than scattered inputs to the new CEO. The board has to have the same candor in discussions after the successor is chosen. If the new CEO is stumbling, for example, coaching and other kinds of support may help. But the board can't rule out the possibility that despite their best efforts, they may have chosen wrong. In any case, succession planning is not a onetime event but rather an ongoing process that must begin anew the day the new CEO comes on board.

Those Who Are Not Called

Disappointment is inevitable when candidates are vying for the CEO's job, and not only for the one or several who lost out. Anyone who hopes to reach the pinnacle of corporate power and is within five to ten years of the newly elected CEO's age probably will never attain their goal in that company. What, then, should the disappointed individuals do about their situation, and is there anything the company should do?

If there are three candidates for the CEO position—an extremely favorable situation for the board—the board and the outgoing CEO may try to mandate that the new CEO take steps to retain the two other contenders, sometimes by making one of them the COO. This is a mistake. If he wishes to stay, fine. But the new CEO should be free to assemble his own team and not have to go through needless turmoil because his former competitors are being forced on him. It is almost certain that the other contenders for the CEO job will leave the company within a year or two no matter what the new CEO does to retain them, if only because headhunters will hotly pursue them. Everyone involved should be intellectually honest about the situation. If the company is developing its leadership talent pipeline correctly, new CEO candidates will begin to emerge in the next few years anyway.

Contemporaries of the new CEO and younger aspirants who were not ready to be candidates in the latest succession have to look carefully at the company, the new CEO, and their own abilities to decide what steps to take. Some will see that if the CEO stays in the job for, say, eight years at a minimum or twenty years at the high end, time will work against them. Some will feel blocked under her leadership and decide to pursue their CEO aspirations elsewhere. Others may decide to settle in. The new CEO should be prepared for both scenarios and pay special attention to keeping the ones who stay motivated by involving them in important aspects of the business that play to their strengths.

Individual leaders have to decide for themselves what is best. Is the new CEO treating you as a partner, sharing responsibilities, and making sure that you are getting the experiences you need to continue your quest for the top? If you're not satisfied by the way your role is unfolding and you feel that you're being shunted off the CEO path, then you will want to move on. But take that step carefully. Not everyone who thinks he's CEO material really is. Evaluate the quality, depth, and diversity of your experience and the outcomes that you delivered to decide if you can realistically expect to obtain a CEO's post somewhere else.

Chapter 8

ADOPTING THE APPRENTICESHIP MODEL

Only a few companies have in place a leadership development process that follows the tenets set forth in this book. General Electric and Colgate-Palmolive are probably the two that come closest. But an increasing number have realized the need for comprehensive leadership development processes and are in various stages of executing them, including Novartis, Thomson, DTE Energy, WellPoint, Inc., Textron, Inc., and Procter & Gamble. All are using some of the Apprenticeship Model's basic principles and methodologies, although none follow it exactly. Indeed, I designed the model in part from my observations of these and other companies as they broke new ground in succession and leadership development. The model does not demand that companies follow it in every detail; it's the principles that ultimately count.

I believe that any company attempting to build a better leadership development program can learn from those who have gone before. Your efforts will almost certainly differ in some fundamental ways. You may be able to move faster, or you may be starting from a better base. But you will surely face some of the same problems that others encounter. Some will be philosophical, some will be cultural, and some will be merely mechanical.

Thus, my final chapter is a real-time glimpse into Textron as it wrestles with the challenges. This inside story is based on my firsthand observation at the company and on discussions with Lewis Campbell, chair, president, and CEO; John Butler, executive vice president, administration, and chief human resources (HR) officer; and Gwen Callas-Miller, executive director of global leadership development and Textron University. It is not a how-to manual. Textron's leadership development process isn't the same as Colgate's or GE's or any other company. Yours won't be either because you will design it with your own needs and culture in mind. But like the other examples in this book, it will give you useful insights that will guide you as you proceed.

Textron's senior leaders estimate that the company is about 70 percent of the way toward where it wants to be. Most important, leadership development is firmly established in the culture as an imperative for all leaders. "They understand the value," says Callas-Miller. "They know that we want them to have the mind-set that they are teachers." Adds Butler: "Our effort goes down deep as well as across the company. When we define leadership, we're talking about leadership on the plant floor being as important as anywhere else."

Putting Succession and Leadership Development on the Agenda

Founded by Royal Little in 1923 as a small textile company, Textron became the world's first conglomerate in the 1950s, using the earnings from the textile business to acquire diverse businesses. Today, Textron's products range from helicopters, airplanes, and military weaponry to industrial pumps, golf carts, and lawn and turf equipment. Shortly after he assumed the chairmanship in 1999, Campbell began an effort to fundamentally reshape Textron. Rather than a conglomerate with a portfolio of separate businesses, he and the board determined that Textron would become a streamlined networked enterprise: a business model that would allocate capital, set common goals and processes, and share people more effectively across the spectrum of its varied businesses. One of the fundamental changes would have to be its leadership talent development effort.

"We aspire to be *the* premier multi-industry company, recognized for our powerful brands, world-class enterprise processes, and talented people," says Campbell. "For us to achieve this aspiration, we must have extraordinary talent development and retention across the entire company, around the world. This is particularly important in light of the intensifying global competition for both talent and customers."

Before Campbell began Textron's transformation, succession planning was focused almost exclusively on the seniormost management level, specifically the business unit presidents, key corporate positions, and their immediate direct reports. Talent review amounted to an annual meeting at each business unit with the CEO; the management committee, which includes the chief of HR; and the corporate leader responsible for succession planning. The business unit president and his respective HR leader would present the names and résumés of both staff people and high-potential executives and any issues around their performance in current jobs as well as plans for their next move. There was little cross-pollination of talent among the businesses. Each business unit kept personnel information in-house, rarely sharing it with other units. The information was not only difficult to access but also became outdated quickly. Succession planning was treated as a discrete event. The result: a siloed view of talent, limited focus on internal cross-business development, and a constant search outside the company for talent at all levels.

The shift from a traditional conglomerate to a networked enterprise meant that the company would share processes and policies across all its businesses. A common talent development effort would offer the entire Textron enterprise a way to develop people and facilitate knowledge and culture transfer. Some efforts had been made earlier to get the word out at the corporate level about rising young talent in the businesses, but it rarely amounted to much. The leader of a business would stand up at the annual talent assessment meeting and tell his colleagues, "Here's somebody I want you to know about." But leaders of other businesses rarely followed up by trying to attract that rising young star to their business.

Campbell and other senior executives realized that their vision for the company depended on identifying and cultivating leadership talent throughout the company, not just in individual businesses. They understood that only a companywide program would produce a pool of leaders who would be intimately familiar with all aspects of the company's diversified operations and where those businesses might be headed in the future.

HR provides the framework for the program, with significant input from the business leaders, and serves as its steward. "We develop and facilitate the process at every level of the organization," says Butler. Leadership comes from the HR Leadership Team, which includes all the senior HR people in the company (the corporate office as well as each business has its own HR function). It does not act autocratically, though. "The HR leaders at each business have to be satisfied that the tools and processes are doing what is needed."

Any major corporate initiative will succeed only to the extent that the CEO makes it a clear priority and throws himself personally into the effort. That's what Campbell did, putting himself squarely on the line. For example, when he spoke to Textron executives about the need for them to develop their own leaders, he demonstrated the company's commitment to evaluating rising young stars by having the executives evaluate him with the same criteria. "I had some good scores, and I had others that suggested I had an opportunity to work on a few things," he says. "By using myself as an example for developing and learning, discussion goes beyond abstract and theoretical and becomes real." And because Six Sigma plays a role in Textron's transformation and is part of its leadership development program, he sent a strong signal to the entire company by earning a Green Belt in Six Sigma techniques.

Making Succession and Leadership Development Seamless

One of the most important steps in achieving Textron's goals was to make leadership development a subject of continuous discussion not only at the senior levels of the company but also at every level in each of the businesses. Succession planning would no longer be a discrete annual event. Instead, it would be discussed frequently in a series of mechanisms designed to provide the follow-up and follow-through on previous discussions and plans. Talent was also incorporated into routine discussions about business. Thus, leadership development and succession planning became seamless, with no beginning and no end. "By requiring people in all functions and across all businesses to follow the process, we provided the discipline for leaders at every level to identify and develop talent," says Callas-Miller.

The Apprenticeship Model eschews predetermined competencies in favor of dialogue that develops a portrait of each person as an individual. Textron, however, chose to use a set of competencies to give its leaders a common vocabulary for companywide discussions, not just about a person's hard and soft skills but also how the person manifests leadership qualities. "Competencies are viewed as the visible skills and behaviors that are a part of a person's overall leadership capabilities," says Callas-Miller. "They make it easier to have the discussions from which the real insights about individuals emerge."

To help track and manage the vast amounts of information required, Textron initially relied on Microsoft's ACCESS database program. But as the new process spread throughout the company, the volume of data it generated outstripped the program's capacity. Only recently did the requisite software become available. Although the tools are important, Callas-Miller is clear that they are only a means to an end. "They help a supervisor, a leader, a manager, or a senior executive to sit down and have a discussion on short-term and long-term development plans," she says. "But the tools are just a way to get to the discussion. Our goal is to get to the point where every boss is having effective career discussions and doing evaluations well. They have to use the tools routinely for that to happen."

Those dialogues—a fundamental part of evaluating leaders in the Apprenticeship Model—are starting to take shape. Callas-Miller points out that it takes repetition and practice to develop their full potential. "As we discuss people, we need to ensure that we are being as specific as possible in describing capabilities and development needs. We can have a conversation about someone and think we're talking about the same thing, yet we can find later that we have different frames of reference. We're getting more and more precise in those discussions so that everyone will have the same picture."

As part of this effort, those dialogues are guided by the chief HR officer to keep the focus on talent development. "Any dialogue should be facilitated," says Callas-Miller. "While leaders are sensitive about development discussions, an off-the-cuff remark by a senior leader could have an unintended effect. We keep the discussion focused on a person's development. We aren't determining *whether* the person should be developed, but *how* they should be developed. The minute you make development a scarce commodity, it can have an impact on retention."

In keeping with the tenets of the Apprenticeship Model, Textron makes the development of talent a required competency for any leader. Every supervisor is assessed on his or her ability to "develop others." "We want our managers to have the mind-set that they are teachers," she says.

Breaking Barriers to Leadership Development

When Textron began its transformation journey, putting cross-business, cross-functional teams together was challenging because it required leaders to change the way they thought, to put what is best for the enterprise ahead of what may advantage their particular business. For example, says Callas-Miller, "People have a natural aversion to sharing talent if they think they're going to be disadvantaged by it, either by losing a great person or by getting someone who isn't going to be as successful."

The many examples of successful moves have made people more willing. "We've made significant progress in a short time. Now cross-enterprise teams address every significant initiative. This fosters a networked culture as you begin to meet people from all over the company. The value of that change has been demonstrated, and leaders aren't questioning the need for interaction."

Job mobility is essential for creating the varied experiences necessary for well-rounded leadership growth trajectories. Because of its conglomerate legacy, Textron had to work harder than most companies at this. Apart from overcoming the usual reluctance of leaders to give up their best people and to open up jobs held by leaders whose development has leveled off, it had to deal with such problems as differing compensation rates among the businesses. "Developing leaders through relocation sometimes requires creative solutions to ensure that pay differentials do not become a barrier," Callas-Miller acknowledges. "Our compensation group continuously assesses best practices and is working to find solutions to potential barriers, such as the fact that labor markets are in constant flux and that geography impacts the labor market. We have made excellent progress. Benefits were an issue at first, but now we're all on the same salaried health care plan, and 2007 will be the first time we have only one retirement plan."

One tool that encourages movement is a job-posting system that includes positions in every business and function. Callas-Miller says employees can take more responsibility for their careers through direct access to this type of information. "When people know they can start in one place and then move up into positions in other places, they're more willing to join and stay with the company."

The company also uses programs like Six Sigma to build bridges. Classes are composed of people from all units. Then when leaders master the methodology to become "Black Belts," they are moved around the company, providing their expertise to various operations and also practicing their skills in varied contexts. Both the rising leaders and the managers who nominate them for transfer are enthusiastic about the results. "Black Belts often work outside their business or function for two years, and people are now seeing them get good jobs outside these original areas," says Callas-Miller. "That sends people a message that you can hire people for their potential and ability to adapt, as well as add value to the business or function."

The payoff from increased mobility is evident across the company. For example, one of Textron's businesses, headquartered in the Midwest, has become a top supplier of leadership talent to the rest of the company. Because it can develop leaders and provide opportunities for continued growth in other parts of Textron, the Midwest business has improved its ability to attract and retain new talent. Another unit, made up of several small businesses, has been able to attract leaders from other parts of the company because it can provide experience outside the United States.

Equally important, campus recruiters are getting better results. Textron is still not a well-known brand name at the top business schools, but its recruiters are getting more of their grads now because they can demonstrate its strong emphasis on companywide mobility.

Unfinished Business

At the 70 percent completion mark by its own estimate, Textron can point to a solid list of accomplishments. Today, it is filling almost three-quarters of its top leadership positions with internal talent—up from just a tenth in 2001. It can identify two internal backup candidates for each of the company's 170 top executives. So what remains to be done?

Most leaders are still being moved only as job openings occur, rather than into jobs specifically created to test and stretch their skills. "Going forward, we need to provide a broader range of creative development strategies to stretch and develop capabilities," says Callas-Miller. "This would include well-planned assignments within an individual's current responsibilities to creating a short-term position for a high-potential employee who needs to build on a skill set needed to add greater value. We'll get better at this as we continue to emphasize the idea of enterprisewide talent. Ideally one business will say 'I can provide that experience for somebody' or 'I'll open up a position because I know that person needs that experience.'"

Textron is still working on identification and assessment of high-potential leaders. "We've got to get better at finding them earlier and figuring out what to do with them. We need an approach that gives us an aggressive, active, participatory process," she says, adding that each individual has to assume some responsibility for his or her own career development. "They have to know that they own their careers and are responsible for them." Also on the agenda, she says, is completely integrating the components of talent development, from recruiting to assignments, performance management, education, and succession planning.

But the company is also careful about not moving too fast. "We're growing organically," Callas-Miller says. "Nothing is being imposed. We're developing the process at the same rate that the organization can absorb it to ensure that there is a pull and readiness for the next steps."

There's certainly no question in Campbell's mind that the company is on the right track. "When the complete program is in place and we're really good at developing leaders internally, I expect over 90 percent of management talent to come from the inside," he says. "If we're developing people quickly enough, we will increase retention of our very best people, and we'll be developing more people than we can possibly move up. We'll lose some for sure, but as our reputation for talent development grows, it will become easier to recruit and retain people. When people hear about the ground-breaking things we're doing to transform our business, delight our customers, and grow our people, a career at Textron will be even more compelling."

Can you say the same about your company?

Epilogue

WHAT CAN A LEADER DO?

Individual leaders can and should embrace the Apprenticeship Model—even if their companies don't—and take ownership of their own development. Those who believe they have leadership potential that is undiscovered should take charge of their own learning and development. They should make their own luck.

Think of luck as what happens when an opportunity crosses that matches a person's god-given talents. A leader can create her own luck by figuring out when and where that opportunity lies. Every leader should be looking forward, aware of her specific talent and whether it is being fully utilized and developed. If not, the leader should search for a place where her talent can be used, recognized, encouraged, and developed better than anywhere else. Leaders who are persistent in that search will likely find a match between their talent and the opportunity. That becomes luck.

The search, which will continue throughout your career, is a three-part undertaking. First, you need to identify what your potential is. Then you need to find ways to nurture that potential. Finally, you need to be aware of those things that can derail you as your potential develops.

Identifying your potential requires some introspection and the utmost intellectual honesty. Domain or functional expertise becomes less important than other kinds of leadership capabilities as you rise higher in a company, so although it is a starting point, it does not earn you the right to become a leader. Ask any chief financial officer (CFO), and he will almost certainly tell you that some of the accountants working for him are much better versed than he is in such areas as taxation or ever-changing accounting rules and conventions. A good CFO uses his functional knowledge to know what questions to ask of the experts working for him and to get them to do the things that need to be done.

Measure yourself against the criteria the best companies use to identify leaders. Pay particular attention to your social and business acumen. If you have a natural affinity for people, and especially if you can amplify their energy and channel it toward a common purpose, you may be a high-potential leader. Keep expanding your relationships and put yourself in situations that require you to network outside your comfort zone and to lead a team. As you get the chance to select people for jobs, reflect on the quality of your judgments about people. And practice diagnosing and resolving problems in the group dynamics among people who must work together to get things done.

Be sure you are looking at the big picture of the business. Identifying new ways to stay ahead of the competition is a sign that you are thinking broadly; so is setting goals that are higher than the ones your boss gives you because you can see the potential that lies ahead. If you think you have the ability to find clarity in the face of many variables, get feedback; don't wait for it to be given. Ask anyone in a position to have observed you what you could have done better. What one key variable did you miss? What alternative solution did you fail to consider? Most important, try for a position that has profit-and-loss responsibility.

Once you identify your leadership potential, the question becomes, How do you nurture it? It goes without saying that you need to be in a nurturing environment, one that recognizes the need to help high-potential leaders develop themselves at the right pace and in the right way. Let's say you are a young person embarking on your career. You've already demonstrated in your youth a penchant for leadership, perhaps in sports, scouting, or school. You know you have a drive to grow and learn. What kind of company would you join? Obviously, you would seek the one that will help you realize your potential as quickly as possible, create the ambience where the leaders care enough to identify you, give feedback that is honest, give you experiences to test, and take risks on you as a potential future leader. Given those criteria, you probably can think of a number of companies that you would not want to join today. If you want to become a leader and you are graduating from any of the top twenty schools, would you even bother to interview with the recruiters from the American automotive industry and most of its suppliers?

Let's consider the positive side for a moment. Maybe you are among the young leaders who have the courage and boldness to say, "What an opportunity to join a company whose bond rating is junk and whose press is so negative. I will go in and make a difference." And it is possible that you could.

But if the company's modus operandi is not focused now on identifying leaders like you very early and is not willing to give you the experiences to move faster and to create your own path, you almost certainly will be disappointed. If there's any question in your mind about the culture of a company you're thinking about joining, you should take some time and make some phone calls to friends, alumni of your school, or others who can give you information about the company. Is it on the offensive? Are people moved quickly into responsible positions, or are they required to follow a standard career progression?

You need to continually search for the job in which your talent and potential are likely to be best deployed. If they are not being tapped, don't hesitate to keep searching and moving until you find the right opportunity. Jeff Kindler began his business career as vice president of litigation and legal policy at General Electric after an impressive early law career that included clerking for U.S. Supreme Court Justice William J. Brennan and a partnership at Williams & Connolly. From GE he went to McDonald's Corporation as executive vice president and general counsel. While at McDonald's, he moved into line management as president of the company's Partner Brands, which included such well-known restaurant chains as

Boston Chicken, Chipotle Mexican Grill, and Pret a Manger. He joined Pfizer, Inc., the world's largest research-based pharmaceutical company, in 2002 as executive vice president and general counsel, was named vice chair in 2005, and became chief executive and chair of the board in 2006. Kindler had not only the ability but also the persistence to press beyond his obvious domain expertise as a lawyer to become an accomplished and talented leader at the highest level.

Having embarked on the path to leadership development, you have to be on guard against the things that might derail you. A high-potential leader who could spot opportunities and had a drive to develop new products was frustrated by her company's mantra of cost cutting. The longer she stayed in that situation, the more frustrated she became that she was not getting the chance to test her instincts about pursuing top-line growth. A job, a boss, or a company that isn't the best fit with your talent can derail your development. To recognize this situation before it does lasting damage, you need to listen to your inner voice. You should always be asking yourself, Am I testing my potential to the fullest extent, getting the feedback I need, and making improvements in my CEO nucleus? Don't confuse, as many people do, promotions, rewards, and recognition from real progress in developing your leadership potential. Your inner voice will tell you if the fit isn't right. That's when you need to change your circumstances.

You also have to be sure that an organization's culture is right. Some companies, for example, emphasize their collegial culture. Collegiality is fine, but the word is often a euphemism for indecisiveness. Decisions get made by consensus, so no one gets his feathers ruffled, but conflicts often simmer beneath the surface. Decisions, once made, often are revisited two, three, or even four times. Leaders who value decisiveness often find the process frustrating. If you're in that kind of culture, you'll recognize it. You can probably progress in such a company, but is it the place to realize your full potential? At the other end of the scale is a culture that values aggressive behavior. Bosses relish cutthroat arguments under the guise of "candor." Discussions often become personal and the basis for internal competition. People who speak the loudest often drown out more reasoned voices, and the results are wrong decisions. It isn't likely you can change that kind of culture, and it isn't likely you'll prosper in it. You need to move.

Even after you've found the right fit, you have to constantly be aware of the need to curb excessive narcissism. I know many leaders who claim to be humble, but their humility is just a façade. The fact is that most high potentials have an element of narcissism. They take pride in having a reputation for "killer instincts" and in being deemed "clever." But in their quest for success, they sometimes outrun their own abilities, and then they begin to cut corners, going to extremes and stopping at nothing to achieve their goals. Ask yourself from time to time, "Am I building trust? Is my integrity being questioned?" If trust deteriorates or your reputation for integrity suffers, you will face serious impediments to continuing to develop your leadership potential.

Some readers may at some point have to face the realization that despite their aspirations to leadership, they really don't have the raw talent for it. Their impulses, instincts, and temperament are not appropriate for a leadership role, or their mind just doesn't work that way. Ambition and drive are absolutely necessary—but far from sufficient—qualities to achieve a high-level leadership role in a modern corporation. Without the talent to succeed at high levels, ambition and drive can become negatives. It may take some testing and some brutal honesty to determine whether leadership is truly the best path for you, and if so, what kind of leadership or whether your natural gifts should take you in a different direction. Remember that leadership is a job, not a badge of honor.

The best of all worlds is when you find you have a natural talent for leadership, you adopt the tenets of the Apprenticeship Model in managing your own career, and lo and behold, you land in a company that can't wait to help you grow.

Appendix

BUILDING BLOCKS OF THE APPRENTICESHIP MODEL

For the Individual

Building Block 1

An individual's personal leadership growth and development come from experience coupled with timely feedback from those who can observe him in action over extended periods. He practices religiously and consistently one or two items that will leverage his capability and also innovates—meaning that he finds better ways to do the things he's practicing.

Those items fall into three categories: correcting weaknesses, expanding capacity, and expanding capability.

Capacity is how much a person can do in a given amount of time. When she expands her capacity, she can do more in the same amount of time. Capability describes the quality of what a person can do. Expanding it enables her to do significantly more things.

Building Block 2

Leaders need their bosses to make incisive observations about them and to get further observation from others with whom the leaders interact. The bosses must distill from the observations those one or two items that the candidate needs to practice. Most people will tend to focus on weaknesses, style, personality traits, or a combination of these. This can inhibit the expansion of capacity or upgrading of capability and cannot be allowed to happen. The

Apprenticeship Model is grounded in identifying the specific items that help the candidate increase his capacity and capability in spurts.

High-potential leaders need to understand that the most successful path to growth is to expand in concentric circles. This means that each job they advance to must widen the scope of their core skills in a situation of increasing complexity, ambiguity, and speed. In this way, those core skills—whatever their number—get strengthened and honed. These experiences, in turn, strengthen personality traits such as courage, the willingness to take risks, and the ability to perceive external inflection points of change ahead of others.

Building Block 3

An aspiring young leader who wants to reach the pinnacle of success as a CEO or at least the lofty heights of an executive vice presidency should plan to arrive between the ages of forty-five and fifty. Assuming she starts her career with this goal in mind during her early twenties, she will have only twenty to twenty-five years to reach it. Consequently, every step has to count. It cannot be superficial—another punch in the ticket—but must have depth. The higher you go without deep experience, the harder you will eventually fall. Your success in these jobs must be visible so that when you move on, your organization and successor can see that you left something much better than what you found. Your leadership ability is the product of your experiences, and you should be able to look back on them with pride and a sense of accomplishment.

Building Block 4

A leader is not a great leader if he does not produce great leaders for the future. Your boss may not act like this. You need to demonstrate earnest commitment and the multiplier effect—that is, the more you produce, the more your capability increases.

Building Block 5

Do you have a personal process of growth, one where you proactively work to advance yourself? Make a list of things you can do to create such a process. For example:

- I will talk to my boss half a dozen times a year.
- I will seek feedback from three peers and any others who might be able to give it—for example, after a speech I make outside the company.
- I won't wait for opportunities to get experience but will create them. For example, I will ask to participate in task forces in areas outside my own expertise.
- If my boss or my company can't or won't provide me with the feedback and experiences that will expand my capacity and capability, I will seek another boss or another company.

For the Company

Building Block 1

Every company that wants to excel in the future must recognize that the ultimate competitive advantage is a deep leadership pool where leaders at every level are in tune with external changes and can adapt to the speed and depth of those changes.

Building Block 2

Every boss in the company is required to treat leadership identification and development as a critical part of her job. All bosses will be evaluated on how well they execute this duty and rewarded or moved out of their jobs accordingly. An open system for job posting, valuable in its own right for aspiring leaders, will also reveal a lot about each of the bosses.

Building Block 3

In the leadership development part of his job, each boss commits from 20 to 25 percent of his time to observe candidates and give precise feedback and coaching in real time. He must be incisive and work hard to pinpoint no more than two areas a candidate needs to develop and understand how doing so will rapidly increase her capacity, capability, or both.

Building Block 4

The company must have a process that rolls with rhythm and discipline and is replicable. Is it as rigorous as the financial system?

Building Block 5

Every company wants to put the right people in the right jobs. But in traditional corporate practice, the process centers on the job: When one opens, who's the right person for it? The Apprenticeship Model is the opposite: What's the right job for this high-potential leader? The hardest part of this system is devoting the most energy to the right high-potential leaders and creating a culture where placing an individual in the right job, whether existing or newly created, is paramount.

Building Block 6

Leadership can't be taught in a classroom, but educational experiences—classroom training, voracious reading, rubbing shoulders with others in seminars—can accelerate a leader's growth.

Acknowledgments

The ideas presented in this book are based on decades of observing and working with hundreds of great leaders at all levels, some of whom have allowed me to travel with them on their personal development journeys. I have great respect for them as leaders and as human beings and owe each one of them my deepest gratitude.

I would particularly like to acknowledge the following leaders who were immensely generous with their time, attention, and intellect as I researched and wrote this book: Richard Carrión of Banco Popular; George Francis, Cathy Sinning, and Greg Sudderth of Blue Cross Blue Shield of Michigan; Ian Cook, Bob Joy, and Daniel Marsili of Colgate-Palmolive Company; Larry Steward of DTE Energy; Joe Tucci and Jack Mollen of EMC; Maria Luisa Ferré Rangel of Ferré Rangel Group; Pramod Bhasin of Genpact; Jim Noel of Mercer Delta; Anish Batlaw, Juergen Brokatzky-Geiger, Alex Gorsky, Wendy Suter, Corey Seitz, Dr. Daniel Vasella of Novartis Pharmaceuticals Corporation; Lewis Campbell, John Butler, Gwen Callas-Miller, and Ann Pehle of Textron, Inc.; Dick Harrington and Jim Smith of Thomson; Randy Brown of WellPoint, Inc.; Kathy Bloomgarden; and K. Anders Ericsson. A special thanks to General Electric veterans Jack Welch, Larry Bossidy, and Bill Conaty for all I learned about leadership by watching and talking with them over many years, and to current GE CEO Jeff Immelt, from whom I continue to learn.

I have had the benefit of superb editorial talent to help me clarify my thinking and translate it into words on paper. Doug Sease, Geri Willigan, and Charlie Burck each contributed a unique brand of well-honed editorial expertise. My longtime friend, John Joyce, provided useful input as well. I greatly appreciate their contributions.

The team at Jossey-Bass was professional and supportive at every stage. I owe Susan William and Byron Schneider a special thanks for imagining what this book could be and bringing it to the readers who stand to benefit most from it. Thanks to Rob Brandt, Mark Karmendy, and the rest of the production team, who did excellent work.

My gratitude also to team Dallas: Cynthia Burr, Carol Davis, and Karen Baker, who did their usual but always impressive wizardry to keep me and this project on track.

R.C.

About Ram Charan

Ram Charan is a world-renowned adviser to business leaders and corporate boards, a best-selling author, and an award-winning teacher. He is known for his keen insights into business problems and his real-world practicality in solving them.

Jack Welch has said he is "a huge admirer" of Ram's and notes that Ram has a rare ability "to distill meaningful from meaningless" and is unusually adept at helping companies adopt best practices. He said Ram helped "stimulate his thinking" and that he "loved batting ideas around with Ram."

Fortune magazine said Ram is a "wise man," one of the "most influential consultants alive" and a leading expert in corporate governance. *Business Week* put him in the top five teachers in the United States for in-house executive development programs. *The Economist* referred to Ram as a veteran of CEO succession planning.

For nearly four decades, Ram has advised some of the world's most successful business leaders on far-ranging issues, from corporate governance and CEO selection to changing corporate culture and pursuing organic growth. He has worked behind the scenes at companies such as GE, Verizon, Dupont, and Colgate.

Ram's solutions are highly pragmatic, largely because of his field research approach: observing real-life actions and extracting what works.

Ram is also a prolific writer, having authored or coauthored fourteen books, including *Know-How*, *What the CEO Wants You to Know*, and *Boards That Deliver*. *Execution*, written with former

Honeywell CEO Larry Bossidy, was on the *New York Time*'s best-seller list for nearly three years and has two million copies in print. Ram has contributed to lead articles in *Fortune*, *Harvard Business Review*, and many other publications.

Ram's interactive style and practicality have made him a favorite among executive educators. He has taught for thirty consecutive years at GE's John F. Welch Leadership Center in Crotonville, New York, and has won best-teacher awards at Wharton and Northwestern.

Ram's business career started when he was just a teenager, working in the family shoe shop in India. He went on to earn an engineering degree and then master's of business administration and doctorate degrees from Harvard Business School. He graduated from Harvard with high distinction and was a Baker Scholar.

Ram is a director of Austin Industries, Tyco Electronics, and Emaar Manufacturing in India. He was elected a Distinguished Fellow of the National Academy of Human Resources in 2005. He is based in Dallas, Texas.

Index